A Plautus Reader

B̵C **LATIN** Readers
Series Editor:
Ronnie Ancona

These readers provide well annotated Latin selections written by experts in the field, to be used as authoritative introductions to Latin authors, genres, topics, or themes for intermediate or advanced college Latin study. Their relatively small size (covering 500–600 lines) makes them ideal to use in combination. Each volume includes a comprehensive introduction, bibliography for further reading, Latin text with notes at the back, and complete vocabulary. Nineteen volumes are currently scheduled for publication; others are under consideration. Check our website for updates: www.BOLCHAZY.com.

A Plautus Reader
Selections from Eleven Plays

John Henderson

Bolchazy-Carducci Publishers, Inc.
Mundelein, Illinois USA

Series Editor: Ronnie Ancona
Volume Editor: Laurie Haight Keenan
Cover Design & Typography: Adam Phillip Velez
Map: Mapping Specialists, Inc.

A Plautus Reader
Selections from Eleven Plays

John Henderson

Bolchazy-Carducci Publishers, Inc.
1570 Baskin Road
Mundelein, Illinois 60060
www.bolchazy.com

Printed in the United States of America
2009
by United Graphics

ISBN 978-0-86516-694-3

Library of Congress Cataloging-in-Publication Data

Plautus, Titus Maccius.
 [Selections. 2009]
 A Plautus reader : selections from eleven plays / [edited by] John Henderson.
    p. cm. -- (Latin readers)
 Text in Latin with introduction, notes and commentary in English.
 Includes bibliographical references and index.
 ISBN 978-0-86516-694-3 (pbk. : alk. paper) 1. Latin drama (Comedy) 2. Plautus, Titus
Maccius--Criticism and interpretation. I. Henderson, John, 1948- II. Title.
 PA6568.A4 2009
 872'.01--dc22

                                                                    2009043609

Contents

List of Illustrations

Introduction

∞ *1. The Plautus Reader*

The score of comic playscripts by Plautus are the earliest Latin texts we have. They made it through the ancient world to reach ours because they always made people laugh. Gave them plenty to think about *and* a good time. That's why the plays are no trouble to get the hang of, even for beginners: the moves and the verbal jousting are mostly familiar and are where our comic tradition came from, through Shakespeare and Molière, pantomime and music-hall, Zero Mostel in *A Funny Thing Happened on the Way to the Forum* (US) and Frankie Howerd in *Up Pompeii* (UK), and beyond: the great Italian film director, poet, novelist, and playwright Pier Paolo Pasolini directly continued the tradition in Italy with his Plautine *Il Vantone* ('The Bragger') in street dialect. The comedies span a wide range of idioms, extending from the mainstream of saucy adventures in the sex trade with Father as fall-guy-in-chief because he foots all bills, to the trouncing of Bigmouth Trooper by Ms. Hot Stuff; from the fairytale wishes come true of faraway Foundlings fished up on a surprise romantic shore, to the caricature gospel that re-stages the myth of the birth of the Hero, in true panto style, gods and all. Not forgetting the "Drag Queen" Bride.

There is no such creature as a typical Plautus play, but we have chosen excerpts that give a good sense of how a whole script runs, from opening call for hush (**1**) to final bow, and call for applause (**5**)—with two varieties of each. The total count of verses included, short and long, is just over six hundred (616), featuring solos, confrontations and a showcase of fully developed scenes. Two punchy passages present varieties of "metatheater," first speaking out directly to the audience—as directly on-the-nose as any theater in the round ever can—by bringing into the playworld the real venue in the center of Rome; and second discussing, in role, the realities of production and performance (**2**). Next a run of four brisk cameos bring on favorite turns, polishing up fresh versions of old faithfuls, to embody cunning and nonchalance, infatuation and seduction (**3**). The climax comes with five show-stoppers—a pick of extended spectacular stand-outs guaranteed to bring the house down, each given close-up analysis and detailed appreciation (**4**).

All told, the selection will include fifteen passages from eleven plays, ranging from the best- to the least-known: *Amphitryo*, *Asinaria*, *Captivi*, *Casina* (× 2), *Cistellaria*, *Curculio*, *Menaechmi* (× 2), *Poenulus* (× 2), *Pseudolus* (× 2), *Rudens*, *Truculentus*. Between them, they cover the full range of this theater, and the notes and running comments on each passage endeavor to open out onto the plots, themes, and flavor of the scripts at large. Passages are handled in short bursts, all of them between a few and a dozen lines. For each play a **Bibliography** at the foot of each commentary recommends **Editions**, **Translations**, and items for **Further Reading**. An asterisk before an author's *name will refer to works listed in the **General Bibliography** at the end of this **Introduction**. These materials pick out the best in contemporary criticism (in English).

Plautus' **Latin**—what I call "Plautin"—is such a thrill, with so much buzz and edge to it, that you just have to get into the idioms and rhythms. The things he talks about and the way he talks both throw out plenty of challenging colloquial terms and patter; and he mixes up a daring brew of mock Latin verse, with riotously ebullient verbal fireworks, a barrage of witticisms all the way from shrewd to crude, via smart punning and groansome funning. Everyone needs helping along with the language, and so much is happening per sentence that full line-by-line notes on small packets of text set the right pace to secure comprehension and guide enjoyment. At the back of the *Reader*, find a comprehensive **Vocabulary** (together with a **Guide to English Pronunciation of All Proper Names, p. 179**). It wasn't at all hard to choose passages where the Latin runs light on concentrated bursts of outrageously improvised, slang-intensive, or otherwise one-off wordage; but where rare words and odd idioms occur, information is at hand in the notes. The **Vocabulary** does bulk up, but to

a remarkable extent this is down to the proliferation of compound
words: entries indicate word formation, so it is easy to get the feel of
the stock prefixes and take on board their productivity, as in, e.g.:

> **pro-fectō**, *adv.*, for a fact, undoubtedly
>
> **prō-ferō**, **prōferre**, **prōtulī**, **prōlātum**, bring out
>
> **prō-fluō**, **prōfluere**, **prōflūxī**, **prōfluxum**, flow out
>
> **prō-gnātus**, **-a**, **-um**, *past pple. of "defective" verb*, having been
> born from, progeny of (*with abl.*)
>
> **prō-gredior** (**gradior**), **prōgredī**, **prōgressus sum**, walk forward
>
> **pro-hibeō** (**habeō**), **prohibēre**, **prohibuī**, **prohibitum**, hold off,
> keep at bay, prevent, prohibit").

Abbreviations for parts of speech, etc., generally follow the scheme
of *Oxford Latin Dictionary* (ed. P. G. W. Glare, Oxford: Oxford University Press) xxi–xxiii: *adv., adj., interr. pron.*, etc. Technical terms
are given in quotation marks, but need not be internalized: gen. "of
value," "synizesis," etc.

The **Latin Text** is based on the *Oxford Classical Text* of W. M.
Lindsay (1904), but benefits from more recent editions. I include a list
of divergences in **Appendix A (p. 143)**. There is just one short lacuna
in one of the songs; otherwise there are very few problems. I retain
the spelling *quom* for the conjunction *cum*; and the *-o-* in all forms of
uorto; but I assimilate all prefixes (as in *afferō*, etc.). To help read the
play aloud correctly, as verse, I have prepared an electronic version of
the Latin texts of this *Reader* which you will find posted on the web
at http://www.bolchazy.com/pdf/plautusreaderweb.pdf. Here, long
syllables are marked throughout with a makron (as in "cōmoedia");
metrically shortened syllables are marked with a breve (as in "opŭs").
All elided syllables are given in reduced font, except where final *-s*
"prodelides" *es* or *est* (all instances are remarked in the notes). And
I leave a double space where verses have a "main" central caesura, to
help orient the reader to the cadence of the line. One day I hope to see
plays of Plautus regularly marked up in the "contemporary" metrical
style pioneered by A. S. Gratwick, with sublinear dots to mark the

inception of metrical units (as in the Cambridge "Green-and-Yel-low" commentaries by Gratwick on *Men* [**p. 67**] and Christenson on *Amph* [**p. 135**], and in my Wisconsin edition of *Asin* [**p. 99**]); but I know that many readers (students, teachers, academics) find this distracting, as pages bristle and eyes swim. **Translation** is by me.

The *Reader* features passages of Plautus' most common, and most easily assimilated, meters: five in *senarii* and six plus in *trochaic septenarii*; but four songs in mixed meters are also included, since Plautus was a song-and-dance man who turned drama into musical, and to get the overall feel we need a taster of his warbling and cavorting numbers as well as the repartee and set piece turns. **Appendix B,** devoted to **Meter (p. 145)**, explains the two main meters, while outlining the chief metrical forms as they crop up in the course of the songs; the few remaining virtuoso combinations (mainly in anapaests) can run as riotous lyrics without overambitious analysis.

❧ 2. Reading Plautus

To reach the modern world, the twenty-plus scripts under Plautus' joke name provided the Roman Empire with classroom texts and adult reading for fun; they have proved good ever since for learning Latin in every sort of imaginable scenario, as well as passing on patterns and plots for comic theater everywhere. Showbiz for "Flatfoot" (after the clown shoes worn in low-brow Italian farce), "Plautus" had become *the* classic comic scriptwriter for classical Rome when scholars and teachers started drawing up canons and syllabuses a century of touring and revival after his time. Precious little information reached them from his heyday back in the late third and early second centuries BCE, so we have a blank for our author, and of course know virtually nothing for sure about the rough-and-ready, most likely improvised and unscripted, clowning sketches that helped him jazz up the Greek drama his own plays riff and romp away with. None of the classic Greek scripts that he uses and abuses have survived for us to compare, but we have at least a reliable profile for them, in the form of fragments and by triangulation with the treatment they received, a generation after Plautus, from the relatively well-behaved, mainly recited, "character-plays" of Terence, our other survivng Roman comedian. (Like Henderson and Anderson, ha! the two Roman playwrights make a perfect double act, for contrasting "farce" with "comedy of manners": see W. S. Anderson's *A Terence Reader*. Mundelein, IL: Bolchazy-Carducci Publishers, 2009.) The repertoire of Greek comedies they drew on had toured theaters across the Eastern Mediterranean for several generations before Plautus, as companies picked them up from their original production in Athens, through the third and into the second centuries BCE. When they reached Plautus' Rome, these sturdy compositions walked smack into aggressive reconceptualization, and more than met their match (see *Anderson, *Gratwick; and essays in *Segal).

We must presume that the re-designed material went the rounds, way beyond the debut at the state venue (travestied in **1A**, **2A**). In whatever case, the Plautus playhouse we have to imagine will be a temporary open-air affair operating in daylight, with an altar on an otherwise bare stage (**4D**), fronting a triple-door screen that may be activated as, say, a couple of family homes and a sex palace (**3A**), or a home, a temple, and a brothel (**2A**, **4A**). Frequently, mind, we play blind to any central door, and deal, instead, with just two homes (**3C**, **4B**) or one home and a flesh emporium (**1A/2B**, **3B/3D**, **4C**). Exceptionally, intensity can be created by excluding all but a focal home or royal castle (**5A**, **4E**), and it was *possible* for action to move upstairs, and ape tragedy's platform for a spot of grand finale divine condescension (**4E**). Traffic from the wings interweaves with passage through, and repulsion at, the door(s), and when required, business "inside" is fetched out where we can see it (**4A**'s boudoir, **4C**'s party). Besides padding, wigs, funny feet, and so forth, actors wore suitably hammy costumes and masks (**4E**), so you could recognize master and slave but have trouble differentiating whore from daughter (**2B**, **4D**), enslaved master from his identity-swapping slave (**5A**), or god from the human he impersonates (**4E**); and we milk cunning disguise for all it's worth—whether Hooker in a postpartum frock, pregnant Queen, or dreadful drag act Bride (see **4A**, **4E**, **4B**, *Marshall). Props specially featured—besides lantern and travellers' hat, rope and net, plus kit for jolly trawlermen, and a train of looted spoils of war (**4E**; **4D**; **4A**)—star boxes and starlet caskets, to pressurize the path to disclosure: they promise that wherewithal cash and trinket tokens of recognition will, in time, unpack (**3C**, **4D**). Writing materials can hand us a dynamite scene (**4C**), but most of the clowning was done with choreography, for feature songs and soliloquies, or for split-stage aside, eavesdropping, intentionally overheard fooling, ignoring and blanking, and for preening, sauce and derision. Mime techniques putting into physical terms the business of *thinking* must conspire with rhetorical moves when a character *preaches* in our direction—and another pricks the balloon. Specially challenging are routines of threatened violence and defiance, cowing met by cowering; and switching turn-on and put-down on the instant (**4E**; **4A**). No stage directions were provided, beyond the signals and indicators written into the lines, but this just means that the invitation to make the play our own has fewer strings and permits more latitude for the essentials of comedy—down to focus, pace, and timing. And ooh la la. Verse keeps the troupe honest, keeps the show on the road—and makes sure no one in the "Plauthouse" slips into naturalistic, literalistic, unrefracted mode.

For one or two plays, we know when the first grand performance took place; more often we can plug into fit between script and occasion, as when "the pimp's birthday" coincides on stage with "the festival of the goddess of love," while the production was blessing the first celebration of the festival of the freak-out Great Goddess upon the opening of her new temple (**1B**: where the steps provided the seating). When plays regularly act out a party, or at least end on the way to one, we can readily tune into the Holy Day-holiday fizz-buzz of elation and release that animates and emanates from them. Everything about these communal events was proud to be absurdist, as elected officials of the newly emergent superpower of the ancient world sponsored this music-hall musical entertainment slot of over-the-top antics within their programme of city-wide activities: oaths, exclamations, over-emphases, puns, and parody galore. Yet very often the scripts trigger live themes of Roman political sensitivity: return home from victory in the Greek East (**4E**) vs. ransom and rescue of Greek prisoners-of-war (**5A**); lovable children lost and found—the children of *Carthage*, arch-enemy, and victim, of Rome (**2B**). Their geography is overlaid on Roman territory, on world-conquest *as it was happening*, at the heart of Ancient History: the soldier of fortune with treasure looted from faraway battles out in Asia (**4A**); an exile on the coast of North Africa landing *his* Greek "treasure" Sicily-bound (**4D**); twins separated between Sicilian Syracuse and Greek mainland Epidamnus (**3D**). Equally, Plautus makes sure he plunges us into the slutty underbelly of the heaving and teeming Roman cosmopolis, then the fastest-expanding and already vastest conurbation known to the West: hear the parasite's creed (**3B**), let's go to a slave wedding (**4B**), learn how a whore hires a baby (**4A**), help draw up a year's contract for a sex-slave (**4C**). Yet there's room here, too, for magical storm and shipwreck (**4D**), for a guided tour of sleazeball Rome outside the theater (**2A**), and for epiphany from the Roman God Almighty (**4E**). A map of surprises, for an empire where the fun never set.

The plots cut to the quick, cut to the chase. They concentrate on stocking a make-believe vaudeville with all the business of family "soap," where budding young men and misfit grown men who should know better play around with contraband sex-for-sale, pitching romance against finance before wedding and marriage reel them in and back in. Fantasy plotting from the disempowered trickster pits wit against real power-ratios, as slave, or captive, or wife, or incognito stranger (sometimes the "old man/father" himself playing worm turned rebel), upsets the patriarchal system that holds them all fast in the clutches of seriousness, for propriety, routine, anti-life—for The Machine (see especially **3A**, *McCarthy; for theories of comedy, see *Purdie, *Hokenson). Old favorites, walk-on jollity parts and incidental sing-song numbers, do their thing along the way, to inject non-sense and non sequitur into the proceedings so we're kept on our toes between (A) signals of rules torn up (problem) and norms re-established (resolution), and (Z) punctuation with foolery (stunt) and lyricism (hilarity). Along the way, there's time (big time) to mess with the audience, as we watch impossible parables that beam up humanity, peeking out from unlikely places in the social order, only to be mocked for forgetting that what makes a theater comic is the *audience* (see **2A**, *Slater, *Moore). Not everyone will agree, but they're wrong—I am dead sure that these plays keep dishing up *provocations* along with all their self-parodying assurances that all's well (see *Konstan, *McCarthy). For a start, some scripts mock cruelly where others go gooey, and *you* have to work out which; loss of security and identity *blurs* with salvation through recognition; we're *suspicious* when told a comedy may's well be a tragedy and uplift's the order of the day; we hiss the wicked villain but *know* he's us with the repression lifted; "we" disagree, with ourselves, too. Any take-for-granted inertia you can find in "Plautinopolis" will be the bait for the next set-up, count on it. The only thing that's wooden here is the seat you're sitting on (**1A**). Even when I trailer the storylines behind our selection, in the commentaries, don't be fooled: the "action" before you has its own "up front" trap and tease strategies, so wade right in.

These plays famously introduce us, students and academics, "in ya face," to the rogue slaves of Rome, with their loud mouths, streetwise pose, and claim to rule the roost. They get us to meet the rest of the family, and watch the functioning and malfunctioning of the core structure, of parents and children, dependants and hangers-on, and the omnipresent household staff servicing—or running—the show. Problems are cooked up between families, as boys wreck the finances, girls get pregnant, children are rescued from the sex trade. This theater world is a farce, and no transparent window on Rome, but as pimps get cheated, cooks bring on festivities, and jolly fishermen grumble, Plautus does take us on fantasy trips "down" into society—to the red light district, round the city of Rome, and out into the Mediterranean world of believe-it-or-not. His scripts sketch in the essential paradigms of Roman adolescence (and are therefore necessary preparation for reading Latin elegy and other "love poetry": see especially **4A**, **4C**). More widely still, these plays provide crucial scenes for getting to grips with gender, family, and social structure issues (as featured in every program on ancient culture and classical civilization: see *Rei, *Dutsch). For sure, audiences are here to enjoy more of what they like; they come to be surprised. And Plautus has never let them down. This way, fun; this way, Rome.

Right here and now when the Latin fireworks are about to start is where I get to thank the series editor Ronnie Ancona and the press editor Laurie Keenan for all the fun we've had putting the *Reader* together, and to put on record the skill and care they've poured into it. Where I've goofed, those custard pies are for me.

∾ *General Bibliography*

Anderson, W. S. (1993) *Barbarian Play: Plautus' Roman Comedy.* Toronto: University of Toronto Press.

Duncan, A. (2006) *Performance and Identity in the Classical World.* Cambridge: Cambridge University Press.

Dutsch, D. M. (2008) *Feminine Discourse in Roman Comedy. On Echoes and Voices.* Oxford: Oxford University Press.

Gratwick, A. S. (1982) "Drama." In *The Cambridge History of Classical Literature, Volume 2. Latin Literature,* edited by E. J. Kenney and W. V. Clausen (1982), 77–137. Cambridge: Cambridge University Press.

Hokenson, J. (2006) *The Idea of Comedy: History, Theory, Critique.* Madison: Fairleigh Dickinson University Press.

Hunter, R. L. (1985) *The New Comedy of Greece and Rome.* Cambridge: Cambridge University Press.

Konstan, D. (1983) *Roman Comedy.* Ithaca: Cornell University Press.

McCarthy, K. (2000) *Slaves, Masters and the Art of Authority in Plautine Comedy.* Princeton: Princeton University Press.

Marshall, C. W. (2006) *The Stagecraft and Performance of Roman Comedy.* Cambridge: Cambridge University Press.

Moore, T. J. (1998) *The Theater of Plautus. Playing to the Audience.* Austin: University of Texas Press.

Parker, H. N. (1989) "Crucially funny or Tranio on the couch: the *servus callidus* and jokes about torture." *Transactions of the American Philological Association* 119: 233–46 (reprinted in *Segal).

Purdie, S. (1993) *Comedy: The Mastery of Discourse.* Hemel Hempstead: Harvester Wheatsheaf.

Rei, A. (1998) "Villains, wives, and slaves in the comedies of Plautus." In *Women & Slaves in Greco-Roman Culture: Differential Equations*, edited by S. Murnaghan and S. R. Joshel, 92–108. London and New York: Routledge.

Segal, E. ed. (2001) *Oxford Readings in Menander, Plautus, and Terence*. Oxford: Oxford University Press.

Sharrock, A. R. (2009) *Reading Roman Comedy. Poetics and Playfulness in Plautus and Terence*. Cambridge: Cambridge University Press.

Slater, N. (1985) *Plautus in Performance. The Theater of the Mind*. Princeton: Princeton University Press.

Latin Text

∾ 1A Poenulus 1–45

Getting the Audience in on the Act

Enter the PROLOGVS, *in his element as generalissimo.*

1   Achillem Aristarchi mihi commentari lubet:

    inde mihi principium capiam, ex ea tragoedia.

    'sileteque et tacete atque animum aduortite,

    audire iubet uos imperator' — Histricus,

5   bonoque ut animo sedeate in subselliis,

    et qui esurientes et qui saturi uenerint:

    qui edistis, multo fecistis sapientius,

    qui non edistis, saturi fite fabulis;

    nam quoi paratum est quod edit, nostra gratia

10   nimia est stultitia sessum impransum incedere.

    exsurge, praeco, fac populo audientiam;

    iam dudum exspecto, si tuom officium scias:

    exerce uocem, quam per uiuisque et clues.

    nam nisi clamabis, tacitum te obrepet fames.

15   age nunc reside, duplicem ut mercedem feras.

    bonum factum est, edicta ut seruetis mea.

scortum exoletum ne quis in proscaenio

sedeat, neu lictor uerbum aut uirgae muttiant,

neu dissignator praeter os obambulet

20   neu sessum ducat, dum histrio in scaena siet.

diu qui domi otiosi dormierunt, decet

animo aequo nunc stent, uel dormire temperent.

serui ne obsideant, liberis ut sit locus,

uel aes pro capite dent; si id facere non queunt,

25   domum abeant, uitent ancipiti infortunio,

ne et hic uarientur uirgis et loris domi,

si minus curassint, quom eri reueniant domum.

nutrices pueros infantis minutulos

domi ut procurent neu quae spectatum afferat,

30   ne et ipsae sitiant et pueri pereant fame

neue esurientes hic quasi haedi obuagiant.

matronae tacitae spectent, tacitae rideant,

canora hic uoce sua tinnire temperent,

domum sermones fabulandi conferant,

35   ne et hic uiris sint et domi molestiae.

quodque ad ludorum curatores attinet,

ne palma detur quoiquam artifici iniuria

neue ambitionis causa extrudantur foras,

quo deteriores anteponantur bonis.

40   et hoc quoque etiam, quod paene oblitus fui:

      dum ludi fiunt, in popinam, pedisequi,

      irruptionem facite; nunc dum occasio est,

      nunc dum scriblitae aestuant, occurrite.

      haec quae imperata sunt pro imperio Histrico,

45   bonum hercle factum pro se quisque ut meminerit.

∾ *1B Pseudolus 1–2*

Plunging In

Enter the PROLOGVS, *overanddoneinaflash.*

1   exporgi meliust lumbos atque exsurgier:

2   Plautina longa fabula in scaenam uenit.

∾ *2A Curculio 462–86*

Rough Guide to the Roman Forum

Interrupting proceedings, enter the CHORAGVS, *with some tips on the uptown underworld.*

      edepol nugatorem lepidum lepide hunc nactust Phaedromus.

      halophantam an sycophantam magis esse dicam nescio.

      ornamenta quae locaui metuo ut possim recipere;

465   quamquam cum istoc mihi negoti nihil est: ipsi Phaedromo

      credidi; tamen asseruabo. sed dum hic egreditur foras,

      commonstrabo, quo in quemque hominem facile inueniatis loco,

      ne nimio opere sumat operam si quem conuentum uelit,

      uel uitiosum uel sine uitio, uel probum uel improbum.

470   qui periurum conuenire uolt hominem ito in comitium;

     qui mendacem et gloriosum, apud Cloacinae sacrum,

     ditis damnosos maritos sub basilica quaerito.

     ibidem erunt scorta exoleta quique stipulari solent,

     symbolarum collatores apud forum piscarium.

475   in foro infumo boni homines atque dites ambulant,

     in medio propter canalem, ibi ostentatores meri;

     confidentes garrulique et maleuoli supera lacum,

     qui alteri de nihilo audacter dicunt contumeliam

     et qui ipsi sat habent quod in se possit uere dicier.

480   sub ueteribus, ibi sunt qui dant quique accipiunt faenore.

     pone aedem Castoris, ibi sunt subito quibus credas male.

     in Tusco uico, ibi sunt homines qui ipsi sese uenditant,

     in Velabro uel pistorem uel lanium uel haruspicem,

     uel qui ipsi uorsant uel qui aliis ubi uorsentur praebeant;

485   ditis damnosos maritos apud Leucadiam Oppiam ...

     — sed interim fores crepuere: linguae moderandum est mihi.

∽ *2B Poenulus 541–66*

Backstage Onstage

The orphan boy runs the plot: AGORASTOCLES *has his hands full trying to chivvy and drill his waspish* ADVOCATI *for the scam. Watch out, the guy with the girls for hire/sale!*

     AG   nimis iracundi estis: equidem haec uobis dixi per iocum.

     AD   per iocum itidem dictum habeto quae nos tibi
              respondimus.

AG   obsecro hercle, operam celocem hanc mihi, ne corbitam
       date;

       attrepidate saltem, nam uos approperare haud postulo.

545   AD   si quid tu placide otioseque agere uis, operam damus;

       si properas, cursores meliust te aduocatos ducere.

AG   scitis rem, narraui uobis quid uostra opera mi opus siet,

       de lenone hoc, qui me amantem ludificatur tam diu,

       ei paratae ut sint insidiae de auro et de seruo meo.

550   AD   omnia istaec scimus iam nos, si hi spectatores sciant;

       horunc hic nunc causa haec agitur spectatorum fabula:

       hos te satius est docere, ut, quando agas, quid agas sciant.

       nos tu ne curassis: scimus rem omnem, quippe omnes simul

       didicimus tecum una, ut respondere possemus tibi.

555   AG   ita profecto est. sed agite igitur, ut sciam uos scire rem,

       expedite et mihi quae uobis dudum dixi dicite.

AD   itane? temptas an sciamus? non meminisse nos ratu's,

       quo modo trecentos Philippos Collybisco uilico

       dederis, quos deferret huc ad lenonem inimicum tuom,

560   se ut assimularet peregrinum esse aliunde ex alio oppido?

       ubi is detulerit, tu eo quaesitum seruom aduenies tuom

       cum pecunia. AG meministis memoriter, seruastis me.

AD   ille negabit: Milphionem quaeri censebit tuom;

       id duplicabit omne furtum. leno addicetur tibi.

565   ad eam rem nos esse testis uis tibi. AG tenetis rem.

AD   uix quidem hercle, ita pauxilla est, digitulis primoribus.

ॐ *3A Pseudolus 394–414*

The Cunning Slave, or Brains

Slave PSEVDOLVS *must try and think up some action—fast.*

postquam illic hinc abiit, tu astas solus, Pseudole.

395 quid nunc acturu's, postquam erili filio
largitu's dictis dapsilis? ubi sunt ea?
quoi neque parata est gutta certi consili
neque adeo argenti neque — nunc quid faciam scio.
neque exordiri primum unde occipias habes,
400 neque ad detexundam telam certos terminos.

sed quasi poeta, tabulas quom cepit sibi,
quaerit quod nusquam est gentium, reperit tamen,
facit illud ueri simile quod mendacium est,
nunc ego poeta fiam: uiginti minas,
405 quae nusquam nunc sunt gentium, inueniam tamen.

atque ego me iam pridem huic daturum dixeram
et uolui inicere tragulam in nostrum senem;
uerum is nescioquo pacto praesensit prius.

sed comprimunda est uox mihi atque oratio:
410 erum eccum uideo huc Simonem una simul
cum svo uicino Calliphone incedere.
ex hoc sepulcro uetere uiginti minas
effodiam ego hodie, quas dem erili filio.

nunc huc concedam, unde horum sermonem legam.

☙ *3B Menaechmi 77–109*

The Parasite, or Smarm-on-legs—"Greaseball"

Enter PENICVLVS, *everybody's best mate and yours. And his own.*

iuuentus nomen fecit Peniculo mihi,
ideo quia mensam, quando edo, detergeo.

homines captiuos qui catenis uinciunt
80   et qui fugitiuis seruis indunt compedes,
nimis stulte faciunt mea quidem sententia.
nam homini misero si ad malum accedit malum,
maior lubido est fugere et facere nequiter.
nam se ex catenis eximunt aliquo modo,
85   tum compediti anum lima praeterunt
aut lapide excutiunt clauom. nugae sunt eae.

quem tu asseruare recte, ne aufugiat, uoles,
esca atque potione uinciri decet.
apud mensam plenam homini rostrum deliges;
90   dum tu illi quod edit et quod potet praebeas,
suo arbitratu affatim quotidie,
numquam edepol fugiet, tam etsi capital fecerit.
facile asseruabis, dum eo uinclo uincies:
ita istaec nimis lenta uincla sunt escaria.
95   quam magis extendas, tanto astringunt artius.

nam ego ad Menaechmum hunc eo, quo iam diu
sum iudicatus; ultro eo ut me uinciat.
nam illic homo homines non alit, uerum educat
recreatque: nullus melius medicinam facit.

100   ita est adulescens ipsus; escae maxumae
      Cerealis cenas dat, ita mensas exstruit,
      tantas struices concinnat patinarias:
      standum est in lecto, si quid de summo petas.

      sed mi interuallum iam hos dies multos fuit:
105   domi domitus sum usque cum caris meis.
      nam neque edo neque emo nisi quod est carissumum.
      id quoque iam cari qui instruontur deserunt.
      nunc ad eum inuiso. sed aperitur ostium:
      Menaechmum eccum ipsum uideo, progreditur foras.

⁓ *3C Cistellaria 203–29*
Teenager in Love: The Loverboy
ALCESIMARCHVS *sings the blues:"Love hurts."*

203   credo ego Amorem primum apud homines carnuficinam
          commentum.
      hanc ego de me coniecturam domi facio, ni foris quaeram,
205   qui omnes homines supero, antideo cruciabilitatibus animi.

      iactor, crucior, agitor,
      stimulor, uorsor
      in amoris rota, miser exanimor,
      feror differor distrahor, diripior,
210   ita nubilam mentem animi habeo.
211+212 ubi sum, ibi non sum, ubi non sum, ibi est animus,
      ita mi omnia sunt ingenia;

quod lubet, non lubet iam id continuo,

215   ita me Amor lassum animi ludificat,

fugat, agit, appetit, raptat, retinet,

217+218 lactat, largitur: quod dat, non dat; deludit:

modo quod suasit, id dissuadet,

220   quod dissuasit, id ostentat.

maritumis moribus mecum experitur,

ita meum frangit amantem animum;

neque, nisi quia miser non eo pessum,

mihi ulla abest perdito permities.

225   ita pater apud uillam detinuit

me hos dies sex ruri continuos,

227+228 neque licitum interea est meam amicam uisere misero.

229   estne hoc miserum memoratu?

∾ *3D Menaechmi 351–69*
Drop-dead Gorgeous: The Babe

EROTIVM *does her "Come on in, John" number. Who could refuse her open arms?*

351   sine fores sic, abi, nolo operiri.

352+353 intus para, cura, uide, quod opust fiat:

sternite lectos, incendite odores;

355   munditia illecebra animo est amantum.

amanti amoenitas malo est, nobis lucro est.

sed ubi ille est, quem coquos ante aedis esse aït? atque eccum uideo, qui mihi est usui et plurimum prodest.

item hinc ultro fit, ut meret, potissumus nostrae domi ut sit;

360   nunc eum adibo, alloquar ultro.

animule mi, mihi mira uidentur,

te hic stare foris, fores quoi pateant,

magis quam domus tua, domus quom haec tua sit.

omne paratum est, <...................>ro

365   ut iussisti atque ut uoluisti, neque tibi est

ulla mora intus.

367+368   prandium, ut iussisti, hic curatumst: ubi lubet, ire licet
accubitum.

∾ 4A *Truculentus 482–548*

Outmaneuvered: The Soldier and The Whore

STRATOPHANES *is back from the wars, about to look up the self-employed madame* PHRONESIUM *and her maid* ASTAPHIUM, *with a train bearing gifts from the booty. He has it coming, and here it is.*

ST   ne exspectetis, spectatores, meas pugnas dum praedicem:

manibus dvella praedicare soleo, haud in sermonibus.

scio ego multos memorauisse milites mendacium:

485   et Homeronida et postilla mille memorari pote,

486   qui et conuicti et condemnati falsis de pugnis sient.

488   non laudandust quoi plus credit qui audit quam ille qui
uidet:

pluris est oculatus testis unus quam auriti decem:

490   qui audiunt audita dicunt, qui uident plane sciunt.

non placet quem scurrae laudant, manipulares mussitant,

neque illi quorum lingua gladiorum aciem praestringit domi.

strenui nimio plus prosunt populo quam argute cati:

facile sibi facunditatem uirtus argutam inuenit,

495 sine uirtute argutum ciuem mihi habeam pro praefica,

quae alios collaudat, eapse sese uero non potest.

nunc ad amicam decumo mense post Athenas Atticas

uiso, quam grauidam hic reliqui meo compressu, quid ea agat.

PH   uide quis loquitur tam propinque.   AS   miles, mea Phronesium,

500   tibi adest Stratophanes. nunc tibi opust, aegram ut te assimules.   PH   tace.

quoi adhuc ego tam mala eram monetrix, me maleficio uinceres?

ST   peperit mulier, ut ego opinor.   AS   uin adeam ad hominem?   PH   uolo.

ST   euge, Astaphium eccam it mi aduorsum.   AS   salue ecastor, Stratophanes.

saluom te —   ST   scio. sed peperitne, obsecro, Phronesium?

505 AS   peperit puerum nimium lepidum.   ST   ehem, ecquid mei simile est?   AS   rogas?

quin ubi natust machaeram et clupeum poscebat sibi?

ST   meus est, scio iam de argumentis.   AS   nimium tui simile est.   ST   papae,

iam magnust? iamne iit ad legionem? ecquae spolia rettulit?

AS   erre, nudiusquintus natus ille quidem est.   ST   quid
          postea?

510   inter tot dies quidem hercle iam aliquid actum oportuit.

          quid illi ex utero exitio est prius quam poterat ire in
              proelium?

AS   consequere atque illam saluta et gratulare illi.   ST
          sequor.

PH   ubi illa, obsecro, est quae me hic reliquit, eapse abiit? ubi
          est?

AS   adsum, adduco tibi exoptatum Stratophanem.   PH   ubi
          is est, obsecro?

515 ST   Mars peregre adueniens salutat Nerienem uxorem suam.

          quom tu recte prouenisti quomque es aucta liberis,

          gratulor, quom mihi tibique magnum peperisti decus.

PH   salue, qui me interfecisti paene uita et lumine

          quique mihi magni doloris per uoluptatem tuam

520   condidisti in corpus, quo nunc etiam morbo misera sum.

ST   heia, haud ab re, mea uoluptas, tibi istic obuenit labos:

          filium peperisti, qui aedis spoliis opplebit tuas.

PH   multo ecastor magis oppletis tritici opust granariis,

          ne, ille prius quam spolia capiat, hinc nos exstinxit fames.

525 ST   habe bonum animum.   PH   sauium pete hinc sis. ah,
              nequeo caput

          tollere, ita dolet itaque egomet doleo, neque etiam queo

          pedibus mea sponte ambulare.   ST   si hercle me ex
              medio mari

          sauium petere tuom iubeas, petere haud pigeat, mel meum.

          id ita esse experta es: nunc experiere, mea Phronesium,

          me te amare.

530   adduxi ancillas tibi eccas ex Syria duas,

his te dono. adduce hoc tu istas. sed istae reginae domi

svae fuere ambae, earum patriam ego excidi manu.

his te dono.   PH   paenitetne te quot ancillas alam,

quin examen super adducas, quae mihi comedint cibum?

ST   hoc quidem hercle est ingratum donum.

535   cedo tu mi

istam purpuram.

mea uoluptas, attuli eccam pallulam ex Phrygia tibi.

tene tibi. PH hocine mi ob labores tantos tantillum dari?

ST   perii hercle ego miser. iam mi auro contra constat filius:

etiam nihili pendit purpuram.

                            ex Arabia tibi

540   attuli tus, Ponto amomum. tene tibi, uoluptas mea.

PH   accipe hoc, Astaphium, abduce hasce hinc e conspectu
       Syras.

ST   ecquid amas me?   PH   nihil ecastor, neque meres.
       ST   nilne huic sat est?

ne bonum uerbum quidem unum dixit. uiginti minis

uenire illaec posse credo dona quae ei dono dedi.

545   uehementer nunc mi est irata, sentio atque intellego;

uerum abibo. quid ais? nunc tu num neuis me, uoluptas
       mea,

quo uocatus sum ire ad cenam? mox huc cubitum uenero.

quid taces? planissume edepol perii.

                           sed quid illuc noui est?

❧ *4B Casina 780–854*

Invitation to a Wedding: Comedy Gets Married

Head of household LYSIDAMVS (*never named in the script itself*)
comes out, talking back through the door to his wife CLEUSTRATA,
*inside holding up the wedding-feast interminably. It was a nice day
for a white wedding, a wedding to treasure always . . .*

<table>
<tr><td>780</td><td>LY</td><td>si sapitis, uxor, uos tamen cenabitis,</td></tr>
<tr><td></td><td></td><td>cena ubi erit cocta: ego ruri cenauero.</td></tr>
<tr><td></td><td></td><td>nam nouom maritum et nouam nuptam uolo</td></tr>
<tr><td></td><td></td><td>rus prosequi — noui hominum mores maleficos —</td></tr>
<tr><td></td><td></td><td>ne quis eam abripiat. facite uostro animo uolup.</td></tr>
<tr><td>785</td><td></td><td>sed properate istum atque istam actutum emittere,</td></tr>
<tr><td></td><td></td><td>tandem ut ueniamus luci: ego cras hic ero:</td></tr>
<tr><td></td><td></td><td>cras habuero, uxor, ego tamen conuiuium.</td></tr>
</table>

Enter CLEUSTRATA's *maid* PARDALISCA.

<table>
<tr><td></td><td>PA</td><td>fit, quod futurum dixi: incenatum senem</td></tr>
<tr><td></td><td></td><td>foras extrudunt mulieres.   LY   quid tu hic agis?</td></tr>
<tr><td>790</td><td>PA</td><td>ego eo quo me ipsa misit.   LY   ueron?   PA   serio.</td></tr>
<tr><td></td><td>LY</td><td>quid hic speculare?   PA   nil equidem speculor.
     LY   abi:</td></tr>
<tr><td></td><td></td><td>tu hic cunctas: intus alii festinant.   PA   eo.</td></tr>
</table>

Exit PARDALISCA.

<table>
<tr><td></td><td>LY</td><td>abi hinc sis ergo, pessumarum pessuma. —</td></tr>
<tr><td></td><td></td><td>iamne abiit illaec? dicere hic quiduis licet:</td></tr>
<tr><td>795</td><td></td><td>qui amat, tamen hercle, si esurit, nullum esurit.</td></tr>
</table>

sed eccum progreditur cum corona et lampade

meus socius, compar, commaritus, uilicus.

Here comes the groom: enter LYSIDAMVS' *hick slave sidekick*
OLYMPIO.

OL   age, tibicen, dum illam educunt huc nouam nuptam
       foras,

      suaui cantu concelebra omnem hanc plateam hymenaeo
       meo,

800   hymen hymenaee, o hymen.

LY   quid agis, mea salus?   OL   esurio hercle, atque adeo
       haud salubriter.

LY   at ego amo.   OL   at ego hercle nili facio: tibi amor pro
       cibo est:

      mihi ieiunitate iam dudum intestina murmurant.

LY   nam quid illaec nunc tam diu intus remorantur
       remeligines?

805   quasi ob industriam, quanto ego plus propero, procedit
       minus.

OL   quid si etiam suffundam hymenaeum, si qui citius
       prodeant?

LY   censeo: et ego te adiuuabo in nuptiis communibus.

LY   +

OL   hymen, hymenaee, o hymen.

LY   perii hercle ego miser: dirumpi cantando hymenaeum licet

810   illo morbo, quo dirumpi cupio, non est copiae.

OL   edepol, ne tu si equos esses, esses indomabilis.

LY   quo argumento?   OL   nimis tenax es.   LY   num me
       expertu's uspiam?

OL   di melius faciant. sed crepuit ostium: exitur foras.

LY   di hercle me cupiunt seruatum.

Enter from home the wedding train: CLEUSTRATA *with*
PARDALISCA *attending her suave slave* CHALINVS (*radiant in
bridal saffron and panto falsies*).

814B   PA   iam oboluit Casinus procul.

815+816   sensim super attolle limen pedes, noua nupta:

sospes iter incipe hoc, uti uiro tuo

semper sis superstes,

819+820   tuaque ut potior pollentia sit, uincasque uirum
uictrixque sies.

tua uox superet tuomque imperium:

uir te uestiat, tu uirum despolies.

noctuque et diu ut uiro subdola sis,

obsecro, memento.

825   OL   malo maxumo svo hercle ilico, ubi tantillum peccassit —

LY   tace.   OL   non taceo.   LY   quae res?   OL   mala
malae male monstrat.

LY   facies tu hanc rem mi ex parata imparatam:

id quaerunt uolunt, haec ut infecta faciant.

829+830   CL   age, Olympio, quando uis uxorem, accipe hanc ab nobis.

OL   date ergo, daturae si umquam estis hodie uxorem.

LY   abite intro.   CL   amabo, integrae atque imperitae huic

impercito.   OL   futurum est.

ualete.   LY   ite iam, ite iam.   CL   ualete.

CLEUSTRATA *re-enters her house with* PARDALISCA *in tow.*

835 LY   iamne abscessit uxor?   OL   domi est: ne time.
                LY   euax,

          nunc pol demum ego sum liber.

          meum corculum, melculum, uerculum. OL heus tu,

          malo, si sapis, cauebis:

          mea est haec. LY. scio: sed meus fructust prior.

840 OL   tene hanc lampadem.   LY   immo ego hanc tenebo.

          Venus multipotens, bona multa mihi

          dedisti, huius quom copiam mihi dedisti.   OL   o,

          corpusculum malacum.

     OL   mea uxorcula —

                              quae res?

845 LY   quid est?   OL.   institit plantam

          quasi luca bos.   LY   tace sis.

          nebula haud est mollis aeque atque huius pectus est.

     OL   edepol papillam bellulam

                                   — ei misero mihi.

     LY   quid est?   OL   pectus mi icit non cubito, uerum ariete.

850 LY   quid tu ergo hanc, quaeso, tractas tam dura manu?

          at mihi, qui belle hanc tracto, non bellum facit.

          uah.   OL   quid negoti est?   LY   obsecro, ut ualentula
                est,

          paene exposiuit cubito. OL cubitum ergo ire uolt.

     LY   quin imus ergo?   OL   i, belle belliatula.

Exeunt into next door.

ᛰ *4C Asinaria 746–809*

The Foolproof Contract: Scriptwriting Onstage

Loverboy DIABOLVS *has his pal the* PARASITVS *draw up a contract with Madame, for a year's exclusive rights to her "daughter," cash down. It's trickier than it sounds. You'll see, as they read over his draft.*

	DI	agedum istum ostende quem conscripsti syngraphum
		inter me et amicum et lenam. leges pellege.
		nam tu poeta es prorsus ad eam rem unicus.
	PA	horrescet faxo lena, leges quom audiet.
750	DI	age quaeso mi hercle translege. PA audin? DI audio.
	PA	'Diabolus Glauci filius Clearetae
		lenae dedit dono argenti uiginti minas,
		Philaenium ut secum esset noctes et dies
		hunc annum totum.' — DI neque cum quiquam alio quidem.
755	PA	addone? DI adde, et scribas uide plane et probe.

	PA	'alienum hominem intro mittat neminem.
		quod illa aut amicum aut patronum nominet,
		aut quod illa amicae suae amatorem praedicet,
		fores occlusae omnibus sint nisi tibi.
760		in foribus scribat occupatam esse se.
		aut quod illa dicat peregre allatam epistulam,
		ne epistula quidem ulla sit in aedibus
		nec cerata adeo tabula; et si qua inutilis
		pictura sit, eam uendat: ni in quadriduo
765		abalienarit, quo abs te argentum acceperit,

tuos arbitratus sit, comburas, si uelis,

ne illi sit cera, ubi facere possit litteras.

uocet conuiuam neminem illa, tu uoces;

ad eorum ne quem oculos adiciat suos.

770   si quem alium aspexit, caeca continuo siet.

tecum una postea, aeque pocla potitet:

abs ted accipiat, tibi propinet, tu bibas,

ne illa minus aut plus quam tu sapiat.' DI satis placet.

PA   'suspiciones omnes ab se segreget.

775   neque illaec ulli pede pedem homini premat,

quom surgat, neque quom in lectum inscendat proximum,

neque quom descendat inde, det quoiquam manum:

spectandum ne quoi anulum det neque roget.

talos ne quoiquam homini admoueat nisi tibi.

780   quom iaciat, 'te' ne dicat: nomen nominet.

deam inuocet sibi quam lubebit propitiam,

deum nullum; si magis religiosa fuerit,

tibi dicat: tu pro illa ores ut sit propitius.

neque illa ulli homini nutet, nictet, adnuat.

785   post, si lucerna exstincta sit, ne quid sui

membri commoueat quicquam in tenebris.'
          DI   optume est.

ita scilicet facturam. uerum in cubiculo,

deme istuc, equidem illam moueri gestio.

nolo illam habere causam et uetitam dicere.

790 PA   scio, captiones metuis.   DI   uerum.   PA   ergo ut iubes,

tollam?   DI   quid ni?   PA   audi relicua.
          DI   loquere, audio.

PA   'neque ullum uerbum faciat perplexabile,

neque ulla lingua sciat loqui nisi Attica.

forte si tussire occepsit, ne sic tussiat,

795   ut quoiquam linguam in tussiendo proserat.

quod illa autem simulet, quasi grauedo profluat,

hoc ne sic faciat: tu labellum abstergeas

potius quam quoiquam sauium faciat palam.

nec mater lena ad uinum accedat interim,

800   nec ulli uerbo male dicat. si dixerit,

haec multa ei esto, uino uiginti dies

ut careat.' DI pulchre scripsti. scitum syngraphum.

PA   'tum si coronas, serta, unguenta iusserit

ancillam ferre Veneri aut Cupidini,

805   tuos seruos seruet, Venerine eas det an uiro.

si forte pure uelle habere dixerit,

tot noctes reddat spurcas quot pure habuerit.'

haec sunt non nugae, non enim mortualia.

DI   placent profecto leges. sequere intro.   PA   sequor.

❧ 4D Rudens 938–1044
The Tug of War: Finders and Keepers

Slave TRACHALIO, *here with his master on a mission, catches local slave and fisherman* GRIPVS *with a strange catch that—miraculously—he can recognize from way off the beach. There's plenty riding on safe recovery of the contents.*

TR heus, mane.   GR   quid maneam?   TR   dum hanc
        tibi,

            quam trahis, rudentem complico.

GR mitte modo.   TR   at pol ego te adiuuo.

                                nam bonis
            quod bene fit haud perit.

940 GR turbida tempestas heri fuit,

        nil habeo, adulescens, piscium,

                        ne tu mihi esse postules;

        non uides referre me uuidum

                        rete, sine squamoso pecu?

TR non edepol piscis expeto

                    quam tvi sermonis sum indigens.

GR enicas iam me odio, quisquis es.

                    TR   non sinam ego
            abire hinc te. mane.

945 GR caue sis malo. quid tu, malum, nam me retrahis?
            TR audi.

GR non audio.   TR   at pol qui audies post.   GR   quin
        loquere quid uis.

TR eho manedum, est operae pretium quod tibi ego narrare
        uolo.

GR eloquere quid id est?   TR   uide num quispiam
        consequitur prope nos.

GR ecquid est quod mea referat?   TR   scilicet.

950   sed boni consili ecquid in te mihi est?

GR quid negoti est, modo dice.   TR   dicam, tace,

952+953   si fidem modo das mihi te non fore infidum.

954+955 GR do fidem tibi, fidus ero, quisquis es.   TR   audi.

furtum ego uidi qui faciebat;

noram dominum, id quoi fiebat

post ad furem egomet deuenio

feroque ei condicionem hoc
pacto:

'ego istuc furtum scio quoi factum est;

nunc mihi si uis dare
dimidium,

indicium domino non faciam.'

is mihi nihil etiam respondit.

quid inde aequom est dari mihi? dimidium

960   uolo ut dicas.
       GR   immo hercle etiam amplius,

nam nisi dat, domino dicundum

censeo.   TR   tuo
consilio faciam.

nunc aduorte animum; namque hoc omne

attinet ad te.

       GR   quid factum est?

TR   uidulum istum quoiust noui ego hominem iam pridem.
        GR   quid est?

TR   et quo pacto periit. GR at ego quo pacto inuentust scio

965   et qui inuenit hominem noui et dominus qui nunc est scio.

nihilo pol pluris tua hoc quam quanti illud refert mea:

ego illum noui quoius nunc est, tu illum quoius antehac
fuit.

hunc homo feret a me nemo, ne tu te speres potis.

TR   non ferat si dominus ueniat?   GR   dominus huic, ne
frustra sis,

970   nisi ego nemo natust, hunc qui cepi in uenatu meo.

TR itane uero? GR ecquem esse dices in mari piscem meum?

quos quom capio, siquidem cepi, mei sunt; habeo pro meis,

nec manu asseruntur neque illinc partem quisquam
    postulat.

in foro palam omnes uendo pro meis uenalibus.

975   mare quidem commune certo est omnibus.
        TR   assentio:

qui minus hunc communem, quaeso, mi esse oportet
    uidulum?

in mari inuentust communi.   GR   esne impudenter
    impudens?

nam si istuc ius sit quod memoras, piscatores perierint.

quippe quom extemplo in macellum pisces prolati sient,

980   nemo emat, suam quisque partem piscium poscant sibi,

dicant, in mari communi captos.   TR   quid ais,
    impudens?

ausu's etiam comparare uidulum cum piscibus?

eadem tandem res uidetur?   GR   in manu non est mea:

ubi demisi rete atque hamum, quicquid haesit extraho.

985   meum quod rete atque hami nacti sunt, meum
    potissumum est.

TR immo hercle haud est, siquidem quod uas excepisti.
    GR   philosophe.

TR sed tu enumquam piscatorem uidisti, uenefice,

uidulum piscem cepisse aut protulisse ullum in forum?

non enim tu hic quidem occupabis omnis quaestus quos
    uoles:

990   et uitorem et piscatorem te esse, impure, postulas.

uel te mihi monstrare oportet piscis qui sit uidulus,

uel quod in mari non natum est neque habet squamas ne
feras.

GR quid, tu numquam audisti esse antehac uidulum piscem?
TR   scelus,

nullus est.   GR   immo est profecto; ego, qui sum piscator,
scio;

995   uerum rare capitur, nullus minus saepe ad terram uenit.

TR nil agis, dare uerba speras mihi te posse, furcifer.

GR quo colore est, hoc colore capiuntur pauxilluli;

sunt alii puniceo corio, magni item; atque atri.   TR   scio.

tu hercle opino, in uidulum te bis conuortes, nisi caues:

1000   fiet tibi puniceum corium, postea atrum denuo.

GR quod scelus hodie hoc inueni.   TR   uerba facimus, it dies.

uide sis, quoius arbitratu nos uis facere.   GR   uiduli

arbitratu.   TR itan?   GR   ita enim uero.   TR   stultus
es.   GR   salue, Thales.

TR tu istunc hodie non feres, nisi das sequestrem aut arbitrum,

1005   quoius haec res arbitratu fiat.   GR   quaeso, sanun es?

TR helleborosus sum.   GR   at ego cerritus, hunc non
amittam tamen.

TR uerbum etiam adde unum, iam in cerebro colaphos
abstrudam tuo;

iam ego te hic, itidem quasi peniculus nouos exurgeri solet,

ni hunc amittis, exurgebo quicquid umoris tibi est.

1010 GR tange: affligam ad terram te itidem ut piscem soleo
polypum.

uis pugnare?   TR   quid opust? quin tu potius praedam
diuide.

GR   hinc tu nisi malum frunisci nil potes, ne postules.

abeo ego hinc.   TR   at ego hinc offlectam nauem, ne
quo abeas. mane.

GR   si tu proreta isti naui es, ego gubernator ero.

1015   mitte rudentem, sceleste.   TR   mittam: omitte uidulum.

GR   numquam hercle hinc hodie ramenta fies fortunatior.

TR   non probare pernegando mihi potes, nisi pars datur

aut ad arbitrum reditur aut sequestro ponitur.

GR   quemne ego excepi in mari —   TR   at ego inspectaui e
litore.

1020 GR   mea opera, labore et rete et horia?   TR   numqui minus,

si ueniat nunc dominus quoiust, ego qui inspectaui procul

te hunc habere, fur sum quam tu?   GR   nihilo.
TR   mane, mastigia:

quo argumento socius non sum, et fur sum? facdum ex te
sciam.

GR   nescio, neque ego istas uostras leges urbanas scio,

1025   nisi quia hunc meum esse dico.   TR   et ego item esse
aio meum.

GR   mane, iam repperi quo pacto nec fur nec socius sies.

TR   quo pacto?   GR   sine me hinc abire, tu abi tacitus tvam
uiam;

nec tu me quoiquam indicassis neque ego tibi quicquam
dabo;

tu taceto, ego mussitabo: hoc optumum atque
aequissumum est.

1030 TR   ecquid condicionis audes ferre?   GR   iam dudum fero:

ut abeas, rudentem amittas, mihi molestus ne sies.

TR   mane, dum refero condicionem.   GR   te, obsecro hercle,
        aufer modo.

TR   ecquem in his locis nouisti?   GR   oportet uicinos meos.

TR   ubi tu hic habitas?   GR   porro illic longe usque in
        campis ultumis.

1035 TR   uin qui in hac uilla habitat, eius arbitratu fieri?

GR   paulisper remitte restem, dum concedo et consulo.

TR   fiat.   GR   euge, salua res est, praeda haec perpetua est
        mea;

        ad meum erum arbitrum uocat me hic intra praesepis meas:

        numquam hercle hodie abiudicabit ab suo triobolum.

1040   ne iste haud scit quam condicionem tetulerit. ibo ad
        arbitrum.

TR   quid igitur?   GR   quamquam istuc esse ius meum certo
        scio,

        fiat istuc potius, quam nunc pugnem tecum.   TR   nunc
        places.

GR   quamquam ad ignotum arbitrum me appellis, si
        adhibebit fidem,

        etsi ignotust, notus: si non, notus ignotissumust.

ᕚ *4E Amphitruo 361–462*

The Slave Meets His Match: Identity Theft

Slave SOSIA, *bringing back home news of victory, runs into the messenger god* MERCURY, *who has stolen his identity and bars entry to his master's house.*

SO   tun domo prohibere peregre me aduenientem postulas?

ME   haecine tua domust?   SO   ita inquam.   ME   quis erus
        est igitur tibi?

SO   Amphitruo, qui nunc praefectust Thebanis legionibus,

quicum nupta est Alcumena.   ME   quid aïs? quid nomen
tibi est?

365 SO   Sosiam uocant Thebani, Dauo prognatum patre.

ME   ne tu istic hodie malo tvo compositis mendaciis

aduenisti, audaciai columen, consutis dolis.

SO   immo equidem tunicis consutis huc aduenio, non dolis.

ME   at mentiris etiam: certo pedibus, non tunicis uenis.

370 SO   ita profecto.   ME   nunc profecto uapula ob mendacium.

SO   non edepol uolo profecto.   ME   at pol profecto ingratiis.

hoc quidem 'profecto' certum est, non est arbitrarium.

SO   tvam fidem obsecro.   ME   tun te audes Sosiam esse
dicere,

qui ego sum?   SO   perii.   ME   parum etiam, praeut
futurum est, praedicas.

375   quoius nunc es?   SO   tuos, nam pugnis usu fecisti tuom.

pro fidem, Thebani ciues.   ME   etiam clamas, carnufex?

loquere, quid uenisti?   SO   ut esset quem tu pugnis
caederes.

ME   quoius es?   SO   Amphitruonis, inquam, Sosia.
ME   ergo istoc magis,

quia uaniloquo's, uapulabis: ego sum, non tu, Sosia.

380 SO   ita di faciant, ut tu potius sis atque ego te ut uerberem.

ME   etiam muttis?   SO   iam tacebo.   ME   quis tibi erust?
SO   quem tu uoles.

ME   quid igitur? qui nunc uocare?   SO   nemo nisi quem
iusseris.

ME   Amphitruonis te esse aiebas Sosiam.   SO   peccaueram,

nam Amphitruonis socium ne me esse uolui dicere.

385 ME scibam equidem nullum esse nobis nisi me seruom Sosiam.
   fugit te ratio.   SO   utinam istuc pugni fecissent tui.
ME ego sum Sosia ille quem tu dudum esse aiebas mihi.

SO obsecro ut per pacem liceat te alloqui, ut ne uapulem.
ME immo indutiae parumper fiant, si quid uis loqui.
390 SO non loquar nisi pace facta, quando pugnis plus uales.
ME dic si quid uis, non nocebo.   SO   tvae fide credo?
      ME   meae.
SO quid si falles?   ME   tum Mercurius Sosiae iratus siet.
SO animum aduorte. nunc licet mihi libere quiduis loqui.
   Amphitruonis ego sum seruos Sosia.   ME   etiam denuo?
395 SO pacem feci, foedus feci. uera dico.   ME   uapula.
SO ut lubet quid tibi lubet fac, quoniam pugnis plus uales;
   uerum, utut es facturus, hoc quidem hercle haud reticebo
      tamen.
ME tu me uiuos hodie numquam facies quin sim Sosia.
SO certe edepol tu me alienabis numquam quin noster siem;
400   nec nobis praeter med alius quisquam est seruos Sosia,

402 ME hic homo sanus non est.   SO   quod mihi praedicas
      uitium, id tibi est.
   quid, malum, non sum ego seruos Amphitruonis Sosia?
   nonne hac noctu nostra nauis huc ex portu Persico
405 uenit, quae me aduexit? nonne me huc erus misit meus?
   nonne ego nunc sto ante aedes nostras? non mi est
      lanterna in manu?
   non loquor, non uigilo? nonne hic homo modo me pugnis
      contudit?
   fecit hercle, nam etiam misero nunc mihi malae dolent.

quid igitur ego dubito, aut cur non intro eo in nostram
    domum?

410 ME quid, domum uostram? SO ita enim uero. ME quin
    quae dixisti modo

    omnia ementitu es: equidem Sosia Amphitruonis sum.

    nam noctu hac soluta est nauis nostra e portu Persico,

    et ubi Pterela rex regnauit oppidum expugnauimus,

    et legiones Teleboarum ui pugnando cepimus,

415   et ipsus Amphitruo obtruncauit regem Pterelam in proelio.

  SO egomet mihi non credo, quom illaec autumare illum audio;

    hic quidem certe quae illic sunt res gestae memorat
    memoriter.

    sed quid ais? quid Amphitruoni a Telebois est datum?

  ME Pterela rex qui potitare solitus est patera aurea.

420 SO elocutus est. ubi patera nunc est? ME est in cistula;

    Amphitruonis obsignata signo est. SO signi dic quid
    est?

  ME cum quadrigis Sol exoriens. quid me captas, carnufex?

  SO argumentis uicit, aliud nomen quaerundum est mihi.

    nescio unde haec hic spectauit. iam ego hunc decipiam
    probe;

425   nam quod egomet solus feci, nec quisquam alius affuit,

    in tabernaclo, id quidem hodie numquam poterit dicere.

    si tu Sosia es, legiones quom pugnabant maxume,

    quid in tabernaclo fecisti? uictus sum, si dixeris.

  ME cadus erat uini, inde impleui hirneam. SO ingressust
    uiam.

430 ME eam ego, ut matre fuerat natum, uini eduxi meri.

SO   factum est illud, ut ego illic uini hirneam ebiberim meri.

      mira sunt nisi latuit intus illic in illac hirnea.

ME   quid nunc? uincon argumentis, te non esse Sosiam?

SO   tu negas med esse?   ME   quid ego ni negem, qui
      egomet siem?

435 SO   per Iouem iuro med esse neque me falsum dicere.

ME   at ego per Mercurium iuro — tibi Iouem non credere;

      nam iniurato scio plus credet mihi quam iurato tibi.

SO   quis ego sum saltem, si non sum Sosia? te interrogo.

ME   ubi ego nolim Sosia esse, tu esto sane Sosia;

440   nunc, quando ego sum, uapulabis, ni hinc abis, ignobilis.

SO   certe edepol, quom illum contemplo et formam cognosco
      meam,

      quem ad modum ego sum — saepe in speculum inspexi
      — nimis simile est mei;

      itidem habet petasum ac uestitum: tam consimilist atque
      ego;

      sura, pes, statura, tonsus, oculi, nasum uel labra,

445   malae, mentum, barba, collus: totus. quid uerbis opust?

      si tergum cicatricosum, nihil hoc simili est similius.

      sed quom cogito, equidem certo idem sum qui semper fui.

      noui erum, noui aedis nostras; sane sapio et sentio.

      non ego illi obtempero quod loquitur. pultabo foris.

450 ME   quo agis te?   SO   domum.   ME   quadrigas si nunc
      inscendas Iouis

      atque hinc fugias, ita uix poteris effugere infortunium.

SO   nonne erae meae nuntiare quod erus meus iussit licet?

ME   tuae si quid uis nuntiare: hanc nostram adire non sinam.

       nam si me irritassis, hodie lumbifragium hinc auferes.

455   SO   abeo potius. di immortales, obsecro uostram fidem,

       ubi ego perii? ubi immutatus sum? ubi ego formam perdidi?

       an egomet me illic reliqui, si forte oblitus fui?

       nam hic quidem omnem imaginem meam, quae antehac
          fuerat, possidet.

       uiuo fit quod numquam quisquam mortuo faciet mihi.

460   ibo ad portum atque haec uti sunt facta ero dicam meo;

       nisi etiam is quoque me ignorabit: quod ille faxit Iuppiter,

       ut ego hodie raso capite caluos capiam pilleum.

ꙮ *5A Captiui 1029–36*

Clap Now

The CATERVA *wants to hear it for the* CATERVA.

1029   spectatores, ad pudicos mores facta haec fabula est,

1030   neque in hac subigitationes sunt neque ulla amatio

       nec pueri suppositio nec argenti circumductio,

       neque ubi amans adulescens scortum liberet clam svom patrem.

       huius modi paucas poetae reperiunt comoedias,

       ubi boni meliores fiant. nunc uos, si uobis placet

1035   et si placuimus neque odio fuimus, signum hoc mittite:

       qui pudicitiae esse uoltis praemium, plausum date.

❧ *5B Casina 1012–18*

Or Else

Slave CHALINVS *wraps up loose ends—and asks that we show our appreciation for today's play in the usual manner . . .*

spectatores, quod futurum est intus, id memorabimus.

haec Casina huius reperietur filia esse ex proxumo

eaque nubet Euthynico nostro erili filio.

1015 nunc uos aequom est manibus meritis meritam mercedem dare.

qui faxit, clam uxorem ducet semper scortum quod uolet:

uerum qui non manibus clare quantum poterit plauserit,

ei pro scorto supponetur hircus unctus nautea.

Commentary

‹ *1 Enter: The Prologue/Skip the Prologue*

Plautus defies formulae in getting plays started (see *Marshall 194–97). Sometimes he cracks on without a word. And he *can* then fool you by getting back to the preliminaries *after* a lively scene for openers is done. The more elaborate house announcements, program notes, and scene-setting for the plot are specially important to us for the information they provide on Roman theater culture, from Plautus' day and beyond—for some plays make it quite clear that the scripts we are reading have been re-tooled in later productions, and anticipate audiences who love their "good ol' Plautus." **1A** is the classic "Welcome everybody, take your seats, enjoy the show" routine that makes an opening burst of fun out of stage business, and tells us which Romans we are, and are not, supposed to be. **1B** is a muscular version of the minimum fuss approach—"Pin back your ears, and On with the Show."

‹ *1A Poenulus 1–45*

Getting the Audience in on the Act

To tell us to "Sh!" the Prologue conjures up a way to quote a "Sh!" from an extremely unlikely source, a lost play from a lost Greek playwright, a *tragedy* recently adapted (maybe) for the Roman stage. This is followed up in 11–15 by getting the public address man to do his stuff, and hu*sh!* the audience some more. In between, Prologue turns himself into a generalissimo, ready to lick the show into shape for the performance. To get all in place, he wants no scrubbers on stage, no officials mumbling or obstructing the view, no spectators fidgeting or snoring (17–22); no slaves crowding out free citizens (23–27); babies should be home with nursey, respectable wives-and-mothers should pipe down, listen and laugh—but quietly—and save chat for back home (28–31, 32–35); finally, the officials in charge of the festival should see fair play between the rival productions (36–39). Not quite finally, as there's just time to send the squads of slave escorts, who won't be needed till the show is done, off into bottle—to raid a bistro while no one's about, and grab those hot cakes like hot cakes. You can tell this hysterical commander *h*is a regular member of the "Histrio" tribe (4, 44)—not an Istrian from the Balkan coastline opposite Italy, a troublespot periodically "pacified" by Rome, but an *histrio* (actor), and as such, a slave, and so *h*ever so hungry. Which is where he, and we, came in: those who came full were smart; those who came empty will just have to fill up, on fiction, on Plautus' feast of fun (6–10). Because it's a f*ea*stival, there's a holiday show: but, funnily enough, a show's nothing but a slow, masochistic, way to *fast* . . .

So on he'll go, to sell us the plot, or "Plaut" (see **3A**). We, however, will have had an expert run-down on theater-going Rome, gathered in thousands on temporary benches in the city square, or else on the steps of the temple of the god honored by whichever state festival is hosting our first performance. Organizing an audience is both a familiar and an unfamiliar challenge: not so very unlike filling in a legion—of randomly assembled civilians. (For a modern recon-struction of a temporary stage for Roman theater, see **Fig. 1**; cf. **2A**.) The play to come, however, as the play-title "*Little Carthaginian*" al-ready heralds, will be about wars far more vital to Plautus' world than any insubordinate, then victorious, Achilles sacking Troy, as waved to us in the opening line. (In the national legend, Troy was the origin of Rome, through diaspora of refugees.) The Greek script featuring a Father who is combing Greece for his family's long-lost—kidnapped—child hands the Roman playwright a chance to tear us between fellow-feeling for this questing figure's torment, for free, and chauvinistic revelling in mockery of this national enemy. Guilt lurks, too, in the human tragedy inflicted on the ravaged society of *Poen*, by "us," by Rome. We have no information about the circum-stances of the first performance, but the prologue's start with a "mili-tary command" dimension to the play would shout loud as any crier in the context of any games organized to celebrate another success for Roman arms, for world-conquering imperialism (see **4E**).

Fig. 1 A Roman stage set. Replica built by Richard Beacham for his production of *Casina* (**4B**, **5B**) at the Getty Museum, Malibu.

Meter: *senarii* (**p. 146**)

1–10

1   **Achĭllem** here a syllable we might expect to count as long scans short; for the most frequent type, see on 27.

com-mentari this transitive use isn't easy to pin down, but extends the core sense of "applying the mind (*mens*) to" (cf. note on 44–45), to "recall," "rehearse," and (inevitably this is the point) "do a take-off." We're ready for parody re-hash, and it's *not* going to be clear where it stops being quote and where it starts being pastiche and free composition. If you ask Plautus or me, the *whole play* is a pantomime version of "Getting your Child Back from Captivity" tragedies written in the wake of Homer's epic on the doom of Troy, where Greek storytelling *begins*. Not that there ever were any, exactly: but (says Comedy) there *should* have been.

lubet this impers. verb was later spelled *lib-* (so, too, as you know already, with the noun *lubido*).

3   **-que et . . . atque** the overload in connectives (= "polysyn-
      deton") reinforces the redundancy in **silete . . . tacete**; the
      rhetorical triplet, with emphatic length in the third limb (*ani-
      mum aduortite*), hands us a self-contained verse that hams up
      high-style drama to a "t"—except that it claims to be an *actual*
      chunk of tragedy. The last thing we came looking for.

3–5   **animum . . . animo; sedeate in subselliis . . .** *sedeate* is a rare
      2nd person pl. pres. subjunctive form (= -*atis*). The repeti-
      tions continue the repetitiousness of our impresario, drunk
      with power; the same root is doubled in *sedeo . . . sub-sed-lium*
      ("figura etymologica," as already in *prin-cipium capi-am*;
      again at 11, 24–25, etc.); cf. 22, *anim*-; and 15, 18, 20, 23, *sed*-.
      Try hamming up the alliteration on *s* and *d* that threads from
      5 through 35, featuring the "wake-up call" at 21, and you'll be
      in the swing of things.

6   **et . . . et** "both . . . and." supply *uenerint* with both *qui* and
      qui (pf. subjunctive because categorial, "whoever they may be
      who have come").

9   **quoi** this dat. of *quis* (later spelled *cui*) will soon become fa-
      miliar (see 37), along with the gen. *quoius* (later *cuius*), and the
      frequent conj. *quom* (i.e., *cum*; e.g., 27). Here the construction
      is "<for the person> for whom <something> has been readied
      that he may eat, it is *too much* foolishness to . . .".

      quod edit pres. subjunctive, in a purpose clause = "something
      for him to eat"

      nostra gratia "for our sake." Prologue speaks here for the
      whole company.

10   **sessum . . . incedere** a verb "of motion" with the supine (of
      sedeo) expresses purpose: "that <someone> should go to take
      a seat without having had breakfast . . ."; cf. **20**.

      One thing Roman tragedy couldn't do, but Roman comedy regu-
larly did, was to flash up the name of the Greek dramatist of the
original in the prologue (apparently lost from the text of *Poen* at
53), along with plot summary (*argumentum*) and other information.

Part of the joke here is to attribute the needless quote but to finesse the Latin adaptor: so we meet the fifth-century Athenian playwright Arist-archus (whose name just happens to mean "Best-ruler"/*Best Starter*," get it), and not Ennius, in Plautus' day the "Best-Ruler" of Roman poetry across the range, from epic to satire to tragic scripts (see **4E**). From this bit of pretend uplift, our ringmaster gets straight down to business, down to our digestive systems. Let's make him wave expansively to bracket us all, between smart full stomachs and empty buttheads who will have to fill up on *fābulis*, "tales", so not on *făbulis*, "beans," the Roman "popcorn". From West End to Broadway, "this luvvy knows his bosh ain't nosh", "this old stager can tell baloney from polony" (Beans in the auditorium: a fart joke in there? You'd think. Sh!)

11–16

11   **fac . . . audientiam** this is inside-out, "give the people a hearing," when he means "make the people listen," which is the crier's "job" (*fac . . . of-ficium*, 11–12) in theater; he's still playing a mock herald opening up "public" debate in a political assembly or at an epic or tragic gathering of Homeric chieftains (around Achilles and Co., where the *Iliad* gets going?).

12   **exspecto si** "I have been-and-am waiting <to see> if" (indirect question, with subjunctive)

      tuom = *tuum* the original 2nd declension m. and n. nom. in *-os* and *-om* are retained after stems ending in *-u-*.

13   **quam per** post-poning the pre-position ("anastrophe") is more high-and-mighty spiel . . . **-que et** cf. 3.

      uiuis . . . clues "your voice is your living" makes a good verbal fanfare from one actor to . . . another; backed up by *clues*, which means "you are (well-) known" (lit. "you *hear* yourself *called*"), the paradox collapses into good sense, too: a crier *is* his audibility; he must eat like the rest of us, so he's singing for his supper, and we're listening to his voice rumble so we don't have to hear his tummy roar. (*clues* is the best conjecture to correct the manuscripts' *colis*.)

14   **obrepet fames** "hunger will creep up on you"—but this is a
        high-style flourish, with Hunger virtually personified.

Up jumps the crier, with a job to do; down sits the crier. "Pay him
double!" All this standard by-play is Prologue's job. Like us, he wants
to get started; doesn't appreciate the stop-start shuffle he's orches-
trating. Has his own proclamation to proclaim, like a general to his
troops, like a magistrate to a Roman assembly—laying down the law.
His "regulations" (*edicta*) will soon settle down to four-line bursts
of don'ts and don'ts (cue appropriate "no-no" gestures for each *ne*),
because all this is more of the "stop-start" routine that's coming between us and the play we've come for. No one is going to tell Prologue
to get his job done and sit straight back down; today (contrast **1B**),
that would be more than his job's worth!

17–22

17   **ne quis** *scortum* is n., but the referent is a person (likely male
        in this phrase, "clapped-out flesh trade"), hence the switch
        into male (or female) in the pron. Jumbling rough abuse with
        officialese sets the tone right away. Rent boys (or maybe hook-
        ers) and . . .

18   . . . cops! Lictors were attendants provided by the state,
        equipped with canes (and axes) to assert the power of Roman
        magistrates to coerce Joe Public bodily, if need be. "A lictor or
        his cane . . .": you see, a lictor's voice, *his* living, *was* his cane
        (*uerbum*, acc. ~ *uirgae*, nom.; cf. the jingle at 26, *uar*- . . . *uir*-).
        He makes a lousy actor, though—mumbling his lines.

19   **dis-signator** "assigner in different directions (to seats)."
        praeter "in front of, past."

20   **siem, -es, -et, -ent** = *sim, sis, sit, sint*, subjunctive of *sum*; *dum*
        usually takes the pres. indicative, but there is an element of
        "purpose" involved in the reasoning, and these old forms are
        always just right for ending an iambic verse.

21-22 **decet . . . stent** the impers. verb usually takes an infintive or acc. and infinitive; it almost fades to an appositional role here, as the string of jussive subjunctives gathers momentum through 23–25.

dormire temperent Plautus often uses the infinitive (as if it is a verbal noun, "-ing"), where later Latin would use a subjunctive clause, "Tone down the kipping (i.e., cool it = *stop it*)." Cf. 33.

Theaters are all about people knowing (sitting) where they belong, and forgetting about what else is going on; but theaters are also public places, for distraction and unruliness; for pick-ups to cruise, and security guys to swagger; and ushers—ushers must stop ushering before the play can start—then, no more stopping and starting . . . Make your Prologue do some more hand-signals to get the auditorium into his script, pull us in for the performance: 18, *praeter os ob-* puts ob-stacles in our way, just to remove them; all so we will focus on Prologue. And theater aims to capture our attention; at any rate, comedy wants us *awake*. If Prologue isn't spelling out *too* logically how sleepyheads come into it, don't worry: "surely they're ok, *they* can stand, and not mind about sitting: or else, <next time>, they shouldn't oversleep <, these slowcoaches, but come along earlier to get their places>." It's the usual morning start for a performance, in Greece or Rome.

23–27

24-25 **pro capite . . . an-cipiti** *caput* is used in many Latin phrases and formulae to mean a person's claim to count as a person, their social existence—their *life*. At Rome, slaves were told to work hard and true, and earn eventual manumission: *then* they would get to join in, and go to the show. *an-ceps* (*ambi-caput*), "both sides-headed," is another chance to gesticulate a "one, two" (cf. 15), opposing "here, canes" to "rods, there" (in an "A→B←→B←A" pattern, or "chiasmus").

uitent elsewhere a transitive verb, in Plautus, intransitive, with dat.

25-26 **infortunio . . . uarientur** here is the slave-bashing language of ancient comedy: an old-fashioned "euphemism" ("bit of bad luck"), and a mock-aesthetic metaphor ("create a multi-color effect": our "black-and-blue").

27 **curassint** is an "*s*-form" of the verb, used in early Latin for pres. or pf. subjunctive.

minus a final -*s* was weak enough not to register metrically.

Seating regulations were usually heated measures—formal state laws—enforcing privilege and social tiering, but Comedy is intent, instead, on the margins, the aisles, the people at the back, standing-room only. Slaves, then, first because least: no right to be here; they're for it, twiceover, if push comes to shove: here, from those lictors' canes; back home later, from master's lashes, for bunking off to the show and not getting their chores done. The free adult male city strings together its households, to and fro, with its public institutions: Rome is let out to play today! (*domus*, 21, 25, 27, 29, 34.)

28–31

28 **minutulos** "teeny-weeny," babytalk cut from classical Latinity

29 **ut . . . neu . . . ne** we just got the male slaves back home; now we keep the wetnurse slaves home *before* banning them from the show (23). *All* should stay home and *not one* of them come to the theater.

31 **ob-uagiant** "wail in-the-way," a compar. verb found nowhere else in extant Latin

33 **sva** = *sua* is pronounced here as a monosyllable, "*swa*" (by "synizesis")

In Prologue's world, nurses will get thirsty, babies get hungry (cue more right-left hand signals): no good telling *them* to watch, not make a noise (see, they're *not* "*in-fantes*").

32–35

34   **sermones fabulandi** exaggeratedly pompous . . . *sarcasm*: "conversations (consisting) of story-telling" (gen. of the gerund)

The kids "bleat like kids," and so does that other set of less than full members of The Public: respectable married women (the babies' mothers). From all of these non-men a high-pitched whine (*nutri- infanti- minutu- . . . tinnire*; see *Dutsch, esp. 43-5). So women don't speak, they sing-song, they don't watch, they chatter, and though wives can't quite be barred, they're in the way and better off home, like the slaves and children: this comedian will trade their *laughs* for their hush, putting them in an *impossible* position, as he steps forward to play spokesman and ringleader for the *uiri* that (should) own Rome. Both "here" (closed gesture) and "there" (matching open gesture).

36–39

36   **quodque** "and as to (the fact) that . . ."

37-38   **ne . . . iniuria . . . neue ambitionis causa** "neither by wrong-doing (abl.) nor by reason of lobbying" (*causa* following a gen. is an abl. that serves as a prep., "for the sake of")

39   **quo** with subjunctive, to express purpose

The games are all about "taking care" of chores, of the city's "babies" (*curatores* ~ 28, 29, -*cur*-). We don't think there were any prizes or competition between productions in Roman theater, but we *could* be wrong. Either way, Prologue is speaking for and borrowing the authority of the officials in charge, so he can talk big, talk Justice, take the high ground—just for a moment, before . . .

40–43

41   **popina** this word is Italic dialect for "a cooking (place)" (= Latin *coquina*).

43   **scriblitae** slang for "oven-bake" (cf. Greek *kribanites*?), this
      is "cheesy dough" time for real plebeian Latin, piping hot in
      fast-food Rome, then (and for two thousand years) the hug-
      est cosmopolis the world had ever seen. *scriblitae | aestuant* =
      scriblitae is not elided with *aestuant* (= "hiatus").

. . . he crashes down to his proper farcical level, winding up his
orders of the day by getting back to where we came in, with the idea
that a play's running-time ticks by (*dum . . . nunc dum . . . nunc dum
. . .*) in tummy-rumbling time (cf. 6–10). This actor's last command
to the attendants is (as one slave to another) to get on with it, and not
waste quality holiday time with Plautus! Remembering his role of
generalissimo, Prologue organizes "foot-followers" (*pedisequi*) as if
they are infantry (*pedites*, "foot[-soldiers]") for full-scale assault, at
the double, on a hot spot military target (*irruptio* and *occurrite* are
both of them proper army lingo). Will there be nobody there to stop
the smash and grub raid? Has *everyone* gone to see *Poen*?

44–45

44   **pro imperio** "in accordance with (my) command" (returning
      us to 4, *imperator*)

      | **Histrico** the non-Latin *H-* is allowed consonantal value
      (hence hiatus, not elision) and that horrible—histrionical—
      pun, on which the Prologue's "Welcome, y'all" stunt is based,
      is clinched—or buried (cf. 4). Groan, loud as you like.

We were told "bravo—and keep these orders safe" (16, *bonum factum est . . . seruetis*); but now the boss pretends, for his anticlimactic
finale, that he "nearly forgot" to *give* the crucial last command, after
he so methodically sorted out all his troops on parade, ready for—oh
yes—*action*. In between every line, Prologue has been finding polite/
rude ways to tell us to pay attention, remember we're here to remember, *not* to forget, to think well of the fare, and anyhow *think*. Now
he's got (us) this far, licking the audience into shape, it will be time
for him to run (us), at the double, through the details of the plot.

To give the lie of the land, he'll then switch roles and play a similarly goofy "land-surveyor," who winds up by "nearly forgetting" key information, including the promise of a Happy Ending for today's *"Pocket Carthaginian,"* before finally remembering he has to nip off and get into costume (46–128). I'm sure you'll agree he's done a great job in getting us in there with the crowd—and deserves a big hand.

Bibliography: See on **2B (pp. 55–56)**.

∿ *1B Pseudolus 1–2*
Plunging In

This time, there's just time to set the tone, for the "grueling ordeal" (!) of sitting through *another whole play*! Emphasis on physical ambience plugs us straight into the knockabout idiom of Plautine theater. It's a neat twist, for starters, to ditch audience-calming in favor of open incitement to get up and take a stretch while you still can. At least the spectators must be in their seats already if they are to stand up and shake it all about. As for the play for today, I wouldn't go expecting *Pseud* to turn out *specially* "long"—maybe Prologue's kidding (he is) and this is just the first trick on the audience. For the plot, see on **3A (pp. 58–59)**.

Meter: *senarii* (**p. 146**)

1–2

1   **meliust** = *melius est* a final *-s* was weak enough not to register metrically; and the *-e* of *es* and *est* was always so weak that it was regularly overridden by a preceding final syllable ending with a vowel or final *-m* (= "prodelision"). In this *Reader*, expect some instances of *-u's* (= *-us es*) and more instances of *-ust* (= *-us est*).

         exsurgier the archaic pres. pass. infinitive termination in *-ier* (for *-i*) is often used by Plautus to end an iambic or trochaic verse.

Poen menaced us with tragedy, and its pomposity; now we're threatened with a marathon. But we're also being handed a chance to take a wiggle, anyway we feel like doing it: you *can* keep it clean and above the waist, but I would say that *lumbos* licenses me to see you shakin' that ass. In your thousands, of togas (on adult male citizens, but *stolae*, on respectable women, and suitable dress-codes for other social groups).

Bibliography: See on **3A** (**pp. 61–62**).

∾ *2 Theater and Metatheater*

Plautus' playhouse makes no bones about knowing the score. The cast is capable of "stepping forward" at any moment and talking to each other and to the audience, about the city outside the theater-space, or about how the play's going, what it's like being an actor, how to treat an audience. In **2A** the company look beyond the seated spectators to give a guided tour of the lowlife and scum inmates of the Forum. In **2B** a gang of bent "expert witnesses" is being drilled for their role in a frame-up. They know they're cast as "rent-a-chorus"—and remember learning these lines about remembering learning their lines (about . . .) the same place as their hirer/trainer/scriptwriter. The pleasures of such "metatheater" mayhem are the heartbeat of today's critical reception of Plautus.

∾ *2A Curculio 462–86*
Rough Guide to the Roman Forum

This out-of-left-field insert is what we are *not* expecting. As the playlet started, without preliminaries, loverboy Phaedromus was busy explaining to his sidekick slave his so-far chaste love for Planesium, the budding girl for hire from the pimp, "like brother-and-sister." Here in the Greek township Epidaurus, the boy works the girl's old minder over with the magic of wine and song, but that same bewitching night the little spa-town's great healing god Aesculapius refuses to cure the pimp's gutsache. We wait for the play to come to us, hoping to celebrate (as of course we *are*): off in Asia, a soldier-of-fortune planned to buy the girl, via a note authorizing his banker to pay over his deposit to her owner, but the play's livewire, the "parasite" sponger Curculio ("Corn Weevil," a beetle that infests and gobbles flour), got lucky. Sent out there by his host Phaedromus to cadge ("bum") the price of the girl's freedom, he comes home with both nothing and—everything: pissed at a party, the soldier told all, and handed him his chance. He'll play the soldier's aide, complete with eye-patch, and forge the authorization, so as to fool both banker and pimp. (Our interlude cues his return, with Planesium in tow, all paid for.) But he also brings back a certain ring he won dirty dicing with the soldier after dinner, and we'll know why before he's allowed to. The soldier's return will soon shift from threat to godsend, once the girl and he recognize (phew!) they are brother-and-sister, and first banker then pimp are neutralized. A wedding beckons.

So the parasite moved from bit part (like the comic cook) to center-stage, stealing both "Cunning Slave" and "Running Slave" roles-into-one, and gentled *everything* along, wondrously saving the girl for love and for society, by befriending the hulking mercenary, and withholding Aesculapius' balm from just the two villains, that deadly duo of slippery banker and sick and out-of-pocket pimp. Amazingly, however, *Curc* will speak out, loud and clear, across the Roman Forum, through Curculio (506–8):

> . . . You bankers are just the same as pimps:
> At least they take their pitch in under-cover spots:
>> *you* guys operate right in the Forum.
> You carve up people with interest charges:
>> *they* do it with bad pitching and pick-up joints.

So much for any idea that comedy can be sealed off from reality. The whole show sprays its Roman audience with funny Latin, in the full glare of their historic cityscape, and tells them a pretty sight it ain't. Fancy living on an urban filmset, with all these backdrops and characters for hire (464, *ornamenta . . . locaui*)? You do? You do.

Meter: *trochaic septenarii* (**pp. 146–47**)

462–69

462   **ede-pol** "expletive" interjection, "sure, by Pollux!" is a very common intensifier in conversational Latin.

       nactust = *nactus est* (pf. of the deponent verb *nanciscor*, "obtain")

463   **halo-phantam an syco-phantam** understand *utrum eum*, "whether I should say he's a pariah or a liar . . ." The parallel form and sense of this pair of insults from Greek slang (? See **Vocabulary**) are just the job for making no difference which is which. But the second word we're familiar with; the first is murky, and either or both spelling or/and mock-etymology may be being made up by Plautus here and now.

464   **metuo ut** "I'm afraid that I may not . . ."

465   **quamquam** "and yet . . ."

467   **quo in . . . loco** an uncommon postposition of the preposition ("anastrophe")

467-68   **quemque . . . inueniatis, . . . sumat . . . si quem** the change of person, from "you lot (in the audience)" to "someone," is down to the idea of pointing different individuals at individually selected targets. We are promised a discriminating line-up.

468   **conuentum uelit** "should want someone met" (past pple.), i.e., "to meet someone"; a colloquialism common in Plautus.

469   Don't expect to meet any good guys; that isn't what we're here for.

     So, we learn, the "Production Manager" has all the gear on hire (464): will the play's star, Curculio, whose lies just robbed banker and pimp blind, let him have it back after the show? Luckily, Manager lent it on to the Loverboy, so that's *his* problem—along with the rest of the play, all entrusted to his tricksy pal the Parasite. But best to keep an eye on things (466. This Big Brother sounds *just* like the play's Banker). Because this intruder on his own stage-set is *so* extraneous, he could be here to pull any stunt you can think of or dream up; once he's wired us into downtown Rome, it won't ever again be easy to separate off comedy's bunch of fictional reprobates from the real city's characterful heartland. Here money, sex, and lies swirl around the main drain—of Roman social psychology (for the image-repertoire of scum and sludge, see Gowers in **Further Reading** below). Parasite and banker already swapped abuse involving "in*comitium*ing behavior" backed up with "physical per*forum*ation"; and the girl's guzzling minder was even *called* a *cloaca*: *Moore shows in detail how the play tears into the financiers in cahoots with the courts, with a script-wide barrage of aspersions on the Roman business center pilloried here in our inset cameo.

470–85

470   **ito** this 3rd person sing. "jussive subjunctive" (or fut. impera-
       tive) sounds like legal flavoring to get us going to the lawyers'
       center. So too **472** *quaerito.*

472   **ditis** a common contracted form from *dis = diues*

473   **stipulari** it isn't clear whether these "covenanters" are barter-
       ing ("clapped-out rent-boys'") flesh (f)or money.

474   **symbolarum collatores** find "co-contributors to parties"
       ready to chip in for the fish on sale here, staple of both Greek
       and Greek comedy's feasting.

475   **in foro infumo** "at the *bottom* of the Forum" helps to bring
       loaded snobs (literally) down to the gutter. By contrast, "in
       the *middle*," in the full public eye, is a catwalk for "100%
       show-offs" (476).

476   **propter** the spatial sense, "nearby" (from *prope*)

478-79 **qui alteri . . . | et qui ipsi** "both those who . . . at someone
       else (dat. sing.) . . . | and those who themselves." *alter* sug-
       gests abuse swapped between pairs, i.e., one pair of duellists
       at a time.

481   **pone** "behind" (*post-ne*) instantly sounds shady.

483   *Can* we supply a verb (e.g. "You can find") to govern this trio
in acc., and still think it's Latin? Maybe, given the acc. *se-se*
and the parallelism between | *in Tusco uico* . . . , | *in Velabro*
. . . ? Here are the butcher, the baker, the candlestick-maker . . .
—Roman-style, with "the diviner who inspects," not the tea-
leaves, but "the entrails" (*haru-spex*).

484   **uel qui ipsi uorsant uel qui aliis ubi uorsentur praebeant**
these shady dealings with "people either *turning* or else pro-
viding a place for others to *turn*" will be something else to
do with black market *fencing* and/or money-*laundering*, if, of
course, it's not about male-on-male sex (still for cash?).

485   If we aren't phased by *another* dangling acc., *can* we tolerate
the repeat phrase (from/in 472)? And would you let Plautus
mess up his tour good and proper by sticking in a final refer-
ence to some putative unknowable woman on the block? She
would have to be a colorful local character, with a respectable
Roman family name plus an exotique/artsy Greek island place
of origin, and, let's call it, "a residence" to her name (*apud*).
Me, I'm partial to this extra piece to the jigsaw, and *can* find
room in my travesty Forum for this "Happy Blanche's place."
Only just. (Was she a working girl or/then madame—manumitted—*she* says?—by the Oppii?).

These sites would have been in sight, in a northwest to southeast
sweep, if we weren't all crowding round the temporary stage in the
Forum Romanum: see **Fig. 2**; cf. **1A, Fig. 1**.

This main concourse was crossed north to south by the Cloaca
brook (and later main drain), forever flooding; in Plautus' day, the
site of large-scale rebuilding after fire in the Hannibalic War and
rapidly transforming in celebration of successive imperial conquests.
But the mock "human geography" from the management is out to
pin the population of Rome to this, *their* play. Epidaurus' cult of Dr
Aesculapius had been imported to Rome to deal with a plague, and

a temple on the island in the Tiber had been dedicated on January 1st, 291 BCE (while gilded statues would be added in 180); the business of "incubation," sleeping over in the temple in hopes of waking up cured, having visitations, or at least significant dreams for the experts to decipher ("oneiromancy"), was as familiar to Plautus' audience as all the bankers and brothel-keepers, all the soldiers-of-fortune and freeloaders in the world according to Comedy.

486

Since the impresario is acting the part of impresario, he must obey stage rules like the rest of the cast: when "the door creaks," he—and we—will need to hush for the next scene.

Recommended Edition

Wright, J. (1993²) *Plautus' Curculio*, Norman, OK: University of Oklahoma Press.

Translation

Richlin, A. (2006) *Rome and the Mysterious Orient: Three Plays by Plautus*, Berkeley, Los Angeles, and London: University of California Press, 55–108 (supercharged). Or Taylor, H., in D. R. Slavitt and Palmer Bovie, eds. (1995) *Plautus, The Comedies*, 4. Baltimore: Johns Hopkins University Press.

Further Reading

*Moore ch. 7; Gowers, E. (1995) "The anatomy of Rome from Capitol to Cloaca," *Journal of Roman Studies* 85: 23–32.

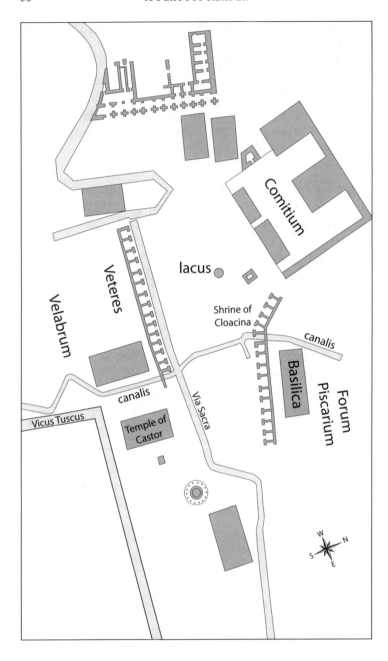

∾ *2B Poenulus 541–66*

Backstage Onstage

Young rascal Agorastocles arrived ahead of his hired band of stooges (at 504), and they've been playing up, insubordinate, and finally standing on their dignity. All just to hold the play up, to rile him, and give us a "chorusline" stunt (like the fishermen's in *Rud*, **4D**). He needs these slowcoach snails sweet. The plan is to bring in a slave unknown in town and invent for him the role of a rich visitor looking for a good time at the local pimp's place: Agorastocles will catch the pimp having stolen his property (slave and money: daylight robbery!) and bring this benchful of witnesses to stitch him up in court, and unload him "tomorrow" (at the *comitium*, cf. **2A**). This is a crummy coup, though, because (as we have already seen, and ogled to a man) "today" is the love-in festival of Aphrodite/Venus, and Agorastocles' girl and her sister are dolled up for the beauty parade/auction of sex slaves—*now*.

In the end, the frame-up will be cloned—re*play*ed—when the combined Forces for Good (= Love) extricate the girls from the pimp's clutches, as freeborn daughters knowingly bought from pirate kidnappers, and challenge him to go to court, see where that

Fig. 2   Map of the second-century BCE Forum, showing: (1) The **Comitium**, a consecrated area reserved for political assemblies and elections, and center of the law courts, at the NW corner; (2) **Shrine of Cloacina**, a small circular platform with two statues, in honor of the goddess of the brook, where it entered the Forum from the north; (3) The **Basilica**, built in the early second century (later developed into the B. Paulli), apparently the place for trade in sex; (4) The **Forum Pisca(to)rium**, the old name for the Macellum, the food market, at the NE, rebuilt in the 170s BCE as an open square surrounded by a portico backed by shops; (5) The **canalis** (= Cloaca Maxima; a winding open culvert, not yet a covered sewer); (6) The **lacus** (Curtius), a spooky Forum monument supposedly marking the spot of a miracle, with some kind of tank to chuck coins in for luck (? Hence paired with the **canalis**?); (7) **Veteres** (Tabernae), once the food shops along the Via Sacra on the south side, now taken over by bankers and moneychangers; (8) The **Temple of Castor**, at the SE corner, where the Cloaca left the Forum, dedicated in 484 BCE and an important meeting-place and rally focus; (9) The **Vicus Tuscus**, the main street leading south, beside the Cloaca, to the Tiber bridge; the home of Roman haute couture, parfumiers, and . . . rent-boys; (10) The **Velabrum**, a patch to south, between the Forum (Romanum) and Forum Boarium, crossed by (9); a busy food market.

gets him. By that time, information supplied by the pimp's alienated
slave has led to the recognition of the boy as well as the girls and to
their reintegration with their Carthaginian "uncle"/father, who has
come to Greek Calydon scouring the planet for the lost children.
Praise be to the gods!

On the way, though, *Poen* is a riot of storytelling botchery featuring a hotch-potch of sideshow vaudeville, misguided plotting,
and para-communication (with plenty of xenophobic messing with
Punic language and culture thrown in). Its "metatheatrical" self-
consciousness *as* "theater" starts from busting the dramatic conven-
tion that foreigners will speak a version of "our" home language (like
all the parts in Roman comedy), extends to creating characters on
stage before our very eyes, and stars "literalistic" interludes playing
up to the real mechanics of the real stage. This in Rome, served up
for Romans glad to have smashed and hamstrung Carthage, soon (?)
to be glad, if on a less spectacular scale, to have done the same for
Calydon in jumped-up Aetolia; and proud, too, of a sexy new temple
of Venus ("Erucina," 181 BCE).

Meter: *trochaic septenarii* (**pp. 146–47**)

541–46

542   **dictum habeto quae** "regard as said . . . the things which . . ."
The pl. items are gathered under a sing. category.

543   **operam celocem . . . ne corbitam date**: "gimme speedboat
help, not some barge!" The noun *c-elox*, "yacht, speed-boat" is
used appositionally, as if it's an adj., displacing its rhyme, the
ordinary adj. *u-elox*, "fast": just so as (not) to be displaced by
its opposite, *c-orbita*, "barge"!

    ne + imperative, "don't . . . ," is frequent in colloquial Latin.

546   **meliust** = *melius est*

So what counts as comic in or out of a comedy? What we agree to read as comic. The boy tries to grease the wheels verbally (543) and claims he's not asking much (just split the difference between the pentasyllabic synonyms *attrepidare* and *approperare*, 544). The cool gang stretch the gap wide again, to two opposed lines-worth, featuring a pair of maddeningly calm words for calm: | *si quid tu placide otioseque agere uis* vs. | *si properas*. He began by ordering "yacht-not-barge"; they trump him with "sprinters-not-lawyers"— *cursores* not (easily confused with) *aduocati*.

547–54

547-49   **opera mi opus siet . . . paratae ut sint** this is the common idiom *opus est* (with abl., and with *ut* and subjunctive), "there is a need (of), it is needful (to)." (*quid* is an emendation, by the scholar Ussing, of the manuscripts' *quod*.)

550   **si . . . sciant** the subjunctive marks a proviso, "supposing that" (= *si modo*).

551   **horunc causa** "for the sake of these people" (gen. pl. masc.)

553   **curassis** the "*s*-form" pres. or pf. subjunctive

554   **tecum una** "at one, together, with you"

The attempt to tick off the plot to be sprung in no time at all is going to backfire (*de . . . de . . . et de . . .*). But first, let's rise to the provocation in that complaint he just couldn't resist slipping in (*tam diu*) with his plea in the name of luv (*me amantem*). Plenty of time for a quibble, about what "knowing" quite means, when it comes to a theater script and concerns the dynamics, not to say the dramatics, of recapitulation (or "re-capping"). It could be argued that what isn't said on stage was never said at all. Moreover, stage action is a matter of acting acting: actors are a special class of agent, and rather than sustaining their own meaningfulness, derive meaning from the way audiences construe them. The particular plot-line ahead, namely: a *plot*, demands due preparation so that the full house can join with the plotters, and not be in the dark like the fall guys. So it's worth taking the time to emphasize that all is indeed, necessarily and rightly, just the way our protagonist initially surmised: "we" *do* "know what's what" (547). But the idea that they know it *because* he "told them," will not wash and cannot pass. This stand-in mock-chorus of a bent posse is not, so it claims (knows?), contrary to many analyses of theater, essentially a dummy audience, representing or channelling our collective response to what we see, feel, or think of the lines we're fed; no, they role-play, too. In their own right. So here we are, putting the cast on the same footing, none of them speakers, or agents, or teachers, all of them learners, actors, and mouthers. Both partners in the crime at present in train are equally in the know, as everyone knows, and nobody needs telling, because this discussion regurgitates and parrots parts about parroting regurgitation. And it's not the fault of these pedestrian pedants if they have had to hold up the acting/action by this action/acting; they have at this stage been obliged to clarify and modify as appropriate the aforesaid prompt to define stage "knowledge" as opposed to staged knowledge and the staging of knowledge. By way of a professionally professed "response." This "hold-up" number is surely bound to get to us.

555–66

557　　**ratu's** = *ratus es* (by "prodelision")

561　　**eo**, "there"

　　　　quaesitum . . . aduenies the supine after a verb "of motion" (again) = purpose.

564　　**addicetur** "will be awarded to you (as your property), handed you on a plate"

"Yes." Yes but no but. This bit of obfuscation obliges the boy in a hurry to check whether the troops do know so that he can know that they know, or whether it's only the troupe that knows etc. etc., and the "you" that matters *haven't* got what's what, which is what counts. Now we've excavated the logic of scriptedness, it's *high time* (another plea: 556, *dudum*) we took our time and took time out to perform competence: I hope "you" will all join in with the invitation to join in with them, and do the "test," the "memory" check, set up for "us" (555, *uos* ~ 557, *nos*). Of course the audience didn't learn their lines before the show opened, but Plautus' crew have rehearsed The Plot carefully enough for us to know the score and sing along with the catch-phrases: "three hundred—" cues "three hundred *Philips* (gold coins = *de auro*)," "Collybiscus the—" spells "villa-guy" (estates manager = *de seruo*), and—got it?— "the pimp—" makes three, for "the pimp is *not* loved by the lover" (= *de lenone*; 548, *amantem* ~ 559, *in-imicum*). All together now?

What the audience *ought* to be "remembering memoriously" (542) is that *they* learned this plot when it was being cooked up and fed *to* Agorastocles, by its inventor, his "Cunning Slave" Milphio (166, 170–86 ~ 558–64). And right now we're twigging ("digging") that the "refinement" promised back then by "Brains" (188–89) was to bring on the *aduocati* for star witnesses—and as such to play first brake, then spare wheel, on the play's cart. To be sure, they *have* "got what's what" (565), as they just witnessed and so did we, and could it *be* any "teeny-tinier finger-tip-size if that"? What isn't at all clear, meanwhile, is how *any* of this fuss and bother is going to hook up with the fancy Carthaginian story that was elaborately promised us back in the Prologue. Except that we spectators are being groomed, to play witnesses against the pimp for detaining property that doesn't belong to him, whether knowingly or not. And teased, mercilessly.

Recommended Editions

Maurach, G. (1975) *Plauti Poenulus*, Heidelberg: Carl Winter is an *editio maior*, in German. Use Nixon, P. (1916) *Plautus*, 4, Loeb Classical Library, Cambridge, MA: Harvard University Press. For a fun student text, with teacher's edition, and video: Brunelle, C., J. H. Starks, Jr., M. D. Panciera (1997) *Latin Laughs: A Production of Plautus'* Poenulus, Wauconda, IL: Bolchazy-Carducci.

Translation

Richlin, A. (2006) *Rome and the Mysterious Orient: Three Plays by Plautus*, Berkeley, Los Angeles, and London: University of California Press, 183–272 (a gas). Or Burroway, J., in D. R. Slavitt and Palmer Bovie, eds. (1995) *Plautus, The Comedies*, 3. Baltimore: Johns Hopkins University Press.

Further Reading

Henderson, J. (1999) "Hanno's punic heirs: Der Poenulus-Neid des Plautus," *Ramus* 23 (= A. J. Boyle ed. [1995] *Roman Literature and Ideology*, Berwick Vic.: Aureal), 24–54 = *Writing Down Rome: Comedy, Satire, and Other Offences in Latin*, Oxford: Oxford University Press, ch. 1. Franko, G. F. (1996) "The characterization of Hanno in Plautus' *Poenulus*," *American Journal of Philology* 117: 425–52. Also Johnston, P. A. (1980) "*Poenulus* I,2 and Roman women," *Transactions of the American Philological Association* 110: 143–59 (cf. *Rei). On the preliminaries, **1B**: Slater, N. (1992) "Plautine negotiations: the *Poenulus* prologue unpacked," *Yale Classical Studies* 29: 131–46 (and *Hunter 25–35). On the "chorus" in **2B**: Lowe, J. C. B. (1990) "Plautus' choruses," *Rheinisches Museum* 133: 274–97.

✂ 3 Four Classic Solos

Here are four of the "stock characters" that the plots re-invent differently each time (see **Fig. 3**). The *Plautus Reader* lines up four of the best to show how this theater works. (For Father, see **4B**; for Soldier, see **4A**.) **3A** and **3B** put side-by-side (1) the chief stand-in on stage for the playwright, the feisty slave who tells those concerned (and us) that he's running the plot, whether he is in charge, improvising wildly, or losing it entirely, always "The Brains" (see **4D**, **4E**; cf. **2B**); and (2) the optional extra, that "friend" who's only around to pick up any crumbs to be had; usually a walk-on part, though sometimes integral to the plot, the parasite specializes in insincerity, bringing a touch of "metropolitan" class to the show: "Smarmy Greaseball"!

Fig. 3   A scene from comedy: Slave confronts Hooker, with sheltering or supporting Youth. A Roman fresco from Pompeii.

(cf. **4C**; **2A**) In **3C** Plautus' "Adolescent" falls for The Wrong Woman; they are all *meant* to, it's part of growing up, and giving everyone else a laugh. Loverboy serenades and comic blues can make for souped-up "musical numbers" at least as good as the real thing (cf. **4C**), because the Plautus experience brought it on, with song and dance plus vaudeville-*loud* repartee, bodily contortions, and other physical buffoonery. **3D** presents the "Female Interest." She can shrink to mere spark for the plot, she can even play déclassée Juliet to Loverboy's Romeo; sometimes she's a long-lost daughter on the brink, or just over the brink, of ruination (see **4D**); other babes range from Grand

Courtesans to working waifs (cf. **4A**). Not knowing which is which is where the tease starts: this time, she's used by the plot, visited by twin brothers and spotting no difference, in the original *Comedy of Errors*. (For other doubles, cf. **4E**.)

∾ *3A Pseudolus 394–414*
The Cunning Slave, or Brains

10th April 191 BCE, the long-promised temple of the "Great Mother" (of the gods: Mater Magna, or Cybele), is dedicated on the south-west Palatine hill, by that year's "mayor of Rome," and Plautus gets to inaugurate the use of the temple steps and apron for theater each Spring with his most upbeat play of all. (*If* we can trust the fragmentary details of the first performance preserved with the script: "*M. Iunio (Bruto), M. fil(io) pr(aetore) urb(ano) ac(ta) Me(galesiis)*, Acted at the Great One's festival when M. Iunius Brutus, son of Marcus, was *praetor urbanus*"). Weird and wonderful, the goddess watches over all. In the script's Athens, it's the up-himself—self-important—pimp Ballio's birthday, on the eve of the town festival of Dionysus, and there's a girl needs saving from his cruel clutches, whips and all. This year, all *his* presents are going out, not coming in. Here's how.

Young Calidorus couldn't raise funds to buy Phoenicium's freedom so she's sold to soldier Polymachaeroplagides, away on campaign, 15 minae down, the balance of 5 due today. But that deal's cancelled if he finds his own 20 first. Since this is farce, slave Pseudolus is allowed to stipulate and formally enounce—as if a Roman gent, whose word was his bond—to both his owner Simo and to the son, in fact to the whole town, and through Simo to the pimp himself, who then warns all his household, to watch out that they're watching out for him, not to "lend to/trust/believe" him (= *credere*), and *still* watch him get the girl from Ballio, plus the 20 minae—from Dad; if he gets the girl, Simo—yes, Simo—will give him, hand over, the money.

Got that? Our clueless/unsinkable hero tells us he suspects we suspect him of not standing to deliver but being out to entertain us, but he'll do it somehow, anyhow. He will find himself pulling it off, only not quite and yet exactly the way Ballio thought he'd be bound to try, by playing Plautus and co-inventing a character to impersonate the guy come from the soldier to collect on the due day. The pimp first takes the balance of 5 minae plus the authorizing letter in exchange for the girl, who's packed off at once; then, sure the danger's over for both of them, he formally promises Simo 20 minae if Pseudolus succeeds, and throws in the girl on top, just for fun. When the soldier's real representative calls on Ballio, he'll want his 15 + 5 minae back in full; because Pseudolus has by then fulfilled his pledge, Simo has a right to the 5 minae that his slave used to dupe the pimp with, and is owed another 20 minae, plus the gift of the girl, on top. But because Pseudolus has now fulfilled his pledge, in that he's already got the girl from Ballio, *Simo* owes *him* 20 minae. Whatever settling up may happen "tomorrow," master and slave split the billroll down the middle, off to join the already swinging party with son and his babe. If we clap, there'll be an invite for us—"tomorrow."

Nothing fazes the conman Pseudolus, who plays such a convincing "Pseudoclueless" in his asides with us, and no doubt the heist is all down to falling on his feet with perfect timing, if it isn't their own projections of devilry suckering the people in charge. Either way, you'll need to concentrate hard to see precisely how the sting worked, or else you'll be the one(s) short-changed. Under pressure, the social sanctions and machinery underpinning interpersonal and commercial confidence buckle spectacularly, as both written authorization and oral public avowal are outflanked by the interplay of brazen bluff with cocksure self-belief at the whip hand. This is the fiendish place comedy comes from. The pimp deserves a round of applause too, mind, for helping to give the goddess a birthday party to go down in histri.

Meter: *senarii* (**p. 146**)

394

394   **illic** = *ille* + the unaccented ("enclitic") particle *-ce* (cf. *illaec*, *illuc*), common demonstrative adj. or pron., "that there (person or thing)"

astas from *ad-sto*

Pitting his wits against the world, "Brains'" soliloquy puts him in the most congenial company for scheming. He is alone with the audience to think it out loud—and get us on his side. Stop the action, the music, the bluffing, and think. Then don't stop when the pace gets up, the heat is on, and there's no time to think.

395–400

395-96 **acturu's . . . largitu's** = *acturus es . . . largitus es*

396 **dapsilis** a Greek adj. (rare after Plautus), here nom. sing., with the jingle *dictis* abl. pl. dependent on it, "plentiful with words"

398 **adeo** "besides"

399-400 **exordiri . . . detexundam telam** two ends of the same metaphor from weaving: "set up the loom . . . weaving off the loom" (*te-la* from *texo*, "web [on a loom]")

"Not a drop" of prefabrication = improvisatory skill ahead? Or else he's trusting to sheer luck? Either way, flying by the seat of his pants—to be judged by results.

401–5

402 **nusquam . . . gentium** colloquial for "nowhere on earth" (a "partitive" gen.)

Here the "metatheatrical" incarnation of the script (and script-writer) by that favorite comic creation, the cunningly sly Slave Trickster, is right up front. Naturally, the money to find won't be real because this is a play—but we're still being given due notice to keep our eyes fixed on the "20 minae." *If* we can . . .

406–8

406 **tragula** a "drag-net," for hunting or fishing
iam pridem "(since) long ago"

408   **nescioquo pacto** "somehow or other" (abl.: lit. "on I-know-not-what term[s]")

The challenge for Pseudolus is high because he's known from before before that he's number 1 suspect, syphoning funds from a canny owner to his son inside one happy family. This *ought* to spark some of his very best work.

409–13

410   **ecc-um** = *ecce-hunc* (cf. -*am*, -*os*, -*as*), demonstrative adj. or pron. common in colloquial Latin, "him" (her/them there)

411   **svo** pronounced as a monosyllable, "*swo*"

The prize is set: "20 minae from master to master's son." And neither he nor we are any the wiser how—"how on earth." But now we know just what to watch who for, where to read the action from, and something about comic timing (the need to pause, hold, then release).

414

414   **legam** "I may pick up"

Wiz is working on the inside track: there were no secrets, with slaves around. Comedy played on that mercilessly. Listen! Whatever next . . .

Recommended Edition

Willcock, M. M. (1987) *Plautus* Pseudolus. Oak Park, IL: Bolchazy-Carducci.

Translation

Smith, P. L. (1991) Plautus, *Three Comedies*, Ithaca: Cornell University Press. Also Watling, E. F. (1973) *Plautus*, The Pot of Gold *and Other Plays*, Harmondsworth: Penguin.

Further Reading

*Moore ch. 5; *Slater ch. 7; Wright, J. (1975) "The transformations of Pseudolus," *Transactions of the American Philological Association* 105: 403–16; Sharrock, A. R. (1996) "The art of deceit: Pseudolus and the Nature of Reading," *Classical Quarterly* 46: 152–74 (repr. in *Segal). On verbal/physical violence in comedy: *Parker.

∾ *3B Menaechmi 77–109*

The Parasite, or Smarm-on-Legs— "Greaseball"

The increasingly plush scene of the Graeco-Roman world sported its own cast of luxury services and city-slickers. One "career choice" was to provide the hanger-on required to help the rich with their conspicuous consumption. In comic scripts, a Parasite was usually an outsize "extra," helping to service the plot rather than develop into a character; instead, he signifies "festivity," like mistletoe—useless, unappealing, but presiding over nice naughtiness.

Meter: *senarii* (**p. 146**)

77–78

77   **iuuentus** the abstract noun is used collectively of the concrete "lads" currently grooving round town, setting the style. The name is dat., agreeing with *mihi*.

Peniculus is a little pun of a pet-name, "Brushkin/Sponge-let," but waves "Prick-let" at us, too; and, in a word, punster culture is the badge of funster adolescence, and post-adolescence. This dude's low-fi verbal hi-jinks set out the comedy stall: gleeful gluttony, brushed-up phallic brag, parasitic parody of all the effort that goes into setting up a feast—*someone else's* effort. When this wag takes his bow, see that his pelvis acts up a bit; that is the thrust of hip jive. It will come true, Plautus means to "clean up" on laughs today, "wipe the floor" with the competition, and make a "clean sweep" of it.

79–86

79-80 **qui . . . et qui** i.e., *ei qui* (*homines captiuos* is object of *uinciunt*) . . . *et qui* . . .

82-83 **homini misero** dat., "for a human wretch," with both *accedit* and *maior lubido est*

85 **anum** the "band" of a metal bond (the diminutive *anulus* is much more frequent, for all manner of "circlet" or "rim"— except the *sphincter ani*)

We expect the wiseguy freeloader to pipe us some verbal icing, and are not disappointed. He's going to over-egg (= overcook) prime comic imagery into daft pontification, so he cues it as such: "Other people are too too daft, in my considered opinion" (81). The Spongeling's glib talk mimes others' bodily suffering, as he "adds pain to pain" by clapping "captured runaways in shackles first, and then fetters" (79–80), which only makes them long to retaliate by "break-out-'n'-freak-out" (83, *fugere-et-facere*); and the actor must find "some way" to repeat this in showing us prisoners "lifting their chains, and filing fetters off their legs or taking a stone to the nail(s)." Parasite is here to talk pedantic rubbish about talking rubbish, and to tell us it, and he, are rubbish, like the nonsense of trying to chain anybody down with irons; and like the nonsense of tying anything down with chains of rhetoric. Broom, broom: "wipe out."

87–95

88 **decet** impers. verb, "it is fitting" (with acc., here the *eum* understood before acc., *quem*, and infinitive, *uinciri*)

89 **homini rostrum deliges** the dat. is an indirect object; we would use gen.: "you can tie down a person's snout." Sarcasm ties human to animal anatomy.

90 **dum . . . praebeas** "provided you provide" (pres. subjunctive: contrast 93)

   quod edit et quod potet both verbs pres. subjunctive to express purpose

91   **suo arbitratu** the reflex. pron. anticipates the 3rd person subject of the main verb *fugiet* ahead: "at his own discretion."

        af-fatim lit. "to saturation" (from obsolete noun, *fatis*)

        quoti-die lit. "on each day." The verse that hands out everything on a plate, in a threefold line-up of adverbial phrases, trips along in 12 syllables (like 88, but all feet iambic)

92   **tam etsi** "although" blurs with "even if"

        capital fecerit "he has/he'll have committed a capital offence" (pf. subjunctive or fut. pf. indicative), in which case "escape" into exile was allowed a Roman citizen.

93   **dum . . . uincies** "so long as you (will) bind" (fut. indicative)

95   **quam magis . . . , tanto . . . artius** "the more . . . , by that much . . . more tightly." The tension between the constructions (displacing either *quanto magis . . .* or *. . . tam magis*) reinforces the "halving" of the verse to ham up Peniculus' conceit: of "food chains" you could "tighten up," and so "bind up" (*extendo = astringo*); but if you do, you also "spread them *out*," and "squash them *in*" (*ex-tendo* vs. *ad-stringo*, *extendo* vs. *artus*). An *extensive* spread *turnsthescrewson* our slave to food.

Here's the thing, then—freebie culture dishing out more comic food for thought. The play brings on a Parasite and a Cook, separately, to start setting up long-lost twin brothers to meet up; but only after *everyone* messes up over which is which, as the new arrival steps straight off the boat and walks into playboy fun-time: his missing half has never really settled, never found himself properly, for all that he's got this new life. Adopted, the waif came into an inheritance, cemented with a marriage-contract; too unfulfilled to grow up, he rows and plays around just like an overgrown kid who's got stuck. So plotting's out today, and we're cued instead to catching up, on the psychological magnetism of family "ties" ("elastic," *lenta*, as any *uincla escaria*), with lashings of verbal and situational irony as the twins' mishaps tally and/yet don't add up. The parasite himself floats free of any real social ties, working the system.

96–99

96   **hunc ... quo** i.e., "the one who lives *here*," (with a waft toward the stage-house door) "to whose place . . ." (lit. "to the place where ")

97   **iudicatus; ultro** the "verdict" has specified the place of detention; the condemned needs no escort, but sets off for "jail"— "voluntarily."

98–99   **alit ... educat ... recreat** "feeds" (as in keeping slaves alive), "takes care of" (as in running the family), "gives them a new lease of life" (as in putting patients back on their feet)

The pace quickens, the imagery flashes by, the plot calls. Soon.

100–103

100–101   **escae maxumae | Cerealis cenas** "feasts like Ceres', with (lit. "[consisting] of") more food than anyone else's." The goddess of cereal crops got a Roman blow-out at her festival each spring.

101–2   **ita mensas exstruit, | tantas struices ... patinarias** the food-junkie's words start "heaping up" great exuberant "dishy heaps" in a burst of grandiosity.

103   **standum est in lecto, si quid de summo petas** the hands are hoisted high, then higher, to measure up "this big . . . , this vast" (*ita, tantas*); then, build—he must step up, from lolling on the couch, beside the spread, and "stand up" tip-toes tall pretending to "go for the eats perched right up top." And—we all fall down; or at least, he must calm down, allowing for a few moments' "interval" before continuing with 104.

The cameo packs in all we want from it to set the tone, whoop it up a little.

104–8A

105   **domi domitus sum . . . deserunt** here's a "meaningless" pun about what means most to Peniculus, inventing the word *domitus* to mean "homey'd" (as if "house-bound"), but to pun on *domitus*, "tamed" (past pple. of *domo*). He paints a nightmare scenario, in which he's "been getting the worst of it, holed up at home with best mates by his side; now, days later, the men are quitting their formations and running out on him: so much for best mates!" Get it? He "buys and bites the matiest stuff going," so he's happy to be "with dear ones," they're "dearest" to him, till they're all gone. (Like Lewis Carroll's Walrus and the Carpenter, and their little friends the Oysters, in *Through the Looking-Glass*, "But answer came there none— | And this was scarcely odd, because | They'd eaten every one.")

So out steps the comedy *we*'ve been waiting ages for. Later, the patron will launch into a gutsy broadside song deploring the Roman social system of patronage, the securing of status by amassing satellite dependants (*clientes*: 571–87). Just what "his" smarmy toady of a hanger-on is turning inside-out here, stingily gorging "on his own" till it's all consumed, and then heading out straight for a host, cynically "feeding on" the proceeds of fake loyalty. Meanwhile the play's stranger in town walks right into a seamy web of hedonistic naughtiness.

108B–9

Little does he know! Abracadabra, in this play you can't spot "Menaechmus himself" for looking, not just because he's an identical twin (and nobody knew it), but because the trick is to have both twins sharing the same name (thanks to a name-switch after one boy was lost from home), and one of *them* unaware of the fact until much confusion has reigned.

Recommended Edition

Gratwick, A. S. (1993) *Plautus* Menaechmi, Cambridge: Cambridge University Press. Student edition, with **Translation** and vocabulary: Lawall, G., and B. Quinn (1978) *Plautus'* Menaechmi, Wauconda, IL: Bolchazy-Carducci.

Translation

Bovie, P., in D. R. Slavitt and Palmer Bovie, eds. (1995) *Plautus, The Comedies*, 4, Baltimore: Johns Hopkins University Press; Watling, E. F. (1973) *Plautus*, The Pot of Gold *and Other Plays*, Harmondsworth: Penguin.

Further Reading

*McCarthy ch. 2; Leach, E. W. (1969) "*Meam quom formam noscito*: language and characterization in the *Menaechmi*," *Arethusa* 2: 30–45; Segal, E. (1969) "The *Menaechmi*: Roman Comedy of Errors," *Yale Classical Studies* 21: 77–93 (repr. in *Segal).

∽ *3C Cistellaria 203–29*

Teenager in Love: The Loverboy

The Boy usually plays the lead, as his adventures carry him from childhood to adulthood, facing the doublespeak of suppression by father spiced with the expectation of breaking out, finding ways around lack of funds and tight surveillance. Somehow he'll wind up married off by his parents. (After all, Dad did, in *his* day.) But there are myriad ways to get there, even if they're almost all called "love." Most of these young "lovers" are playing at emotions, but some get to mean it, and even defy the odds stacked against the "love match" that western modernity standardly insists on. Somehow the Girl would had to have had no previous guys, be recovered for society by recognition as a family-member, and the match approved. A likely story—not! But one is on its way here: look in the *Cist* for the trade secrets it contains, for what's in "the casket" (*cistella*). Another box of tricks from Plautus (cf. **4D**, **4E**; and the fragmentary *Vidularia*, "Trunk-play").

Meter: mixed song (**p. 147**)

203–5

203   **credo ego** announcing a far-fetched "theory" (*coniectura*),
       from the self-engrossed young man in love. All high-falutin'
       stuff, too, wheeling on "The God of Love" himself, invented
       as "inventor of an art amongst humans." A fine way to start
       up the action. Love makes the lover "superhuman," too, be-
       cause (shucks) he beats all mankind in psychic misery. Com-
       edy mixes in just as over-cooked low talk, of meat and tor-
       ture, body and mind: "butchery" or "the torturer's trade" and
       "agony" (*carnuficina* and *cruciabilitas*).

       ni . . . quaeram "if I don't look for," i.e., "not to look for"

This play started with a bang when three women discussed the
love affair between novice girl for hire and our besotted punter or
client, now threatened by his father's intervention as match-maker.
The specially divinized figure "Help" then intervened to help out
by delivering a better late than never prologue and wished revenge
on Rome's Carthaginian enemy, before this solo opened up. We are
promised a song-and-dance of pain to beat all, so prepare to let rip.

206–24

207-8   **uorsor | in amoris rota** in the context (especially *crucior*, "I'm
        racked"), this "wheel of love" images a "rack" for torture. "I'm
        hurledrackeddrivenwhippedspun . . ."

210   **nubilam mentem animi habeo** "I have clouded thinking in
        my heart" (*-i*, locative). Watch the spinning flailing pirouet-
        ting disintegrating ragdoll collapse giddy and faint from ver-
        tigo. He doesn't know where he is, or where he isn't, he's com-
        pletely lost it, and beside himself.

213   **mi omnia sunt ingenia** nothing's making any sense to the
        wreck, and he isn't making much, either: "I've got all the per-
        sonalities going" ("I am legion").

214   **continuo** adv., "straightaway"

215   **lassum animi** "tired in my heart" (-*i*, locative, a second time)

217   **lactat, largitur** "entice" (a rare verb), "lavish (gifts etc.)." Love shuffles desires (214), then wears you out with push and shove, tantalizing and making mock, on-off, off-on.

221   **maritumis moribus mecum experitur** "With me" (i.e., "using me"?) "Love makes an attempt, with the character traits of the sea." More strangulated Latin, but our lover will be dancing the choppy seas of love's character till he's smashed and shattered (222).

223   **nisi quia . . . non eo pessum** "except that I am not going to the sea-bottom"

That's the whole works: "no sort of malady missing from my meltdown" (224). The histrionics have reeled through vivid verb on verb without all the clutter of connectives (= "asyndeton"): ten deponent verbs in a row to start with, four 1st person pres. indicative verbs, plus another twenty-two 3rd person verbs in the indicative, all but two of them pres., all bar one of them sing. This is language under extreme pressure, at once torrential and spasmodic, coming our way in "waves." (For the upbeat swing of "anapaestic" meter, see *Marshall 233–34).

225–29

226   **ruri** the well-to-do family of comedy has a residence in town plus an estate "in the country" (locative).

229   **memoratu** = abl. of the supine, "in recounting", i.e. "to recount".

Yes, all the entrée has *told* us so far has been "Enter *adulescens amator*" (= *miser*, 208, 223, 228, 229). A whole week grounded! Not one visit to his young lady! What counts for comedy is *how* you do the telling.

Recommended Edition

Nixon, P. (1916) *Plautus*, 2, Loeb Classical Library, Cambridge, MA: Harvard University Press.

Translation

Dillard, R. H. W., in D. R. Slavitt and Palmer Bovie, eds. (1995) *Plautus, The Comedies*, 1, Baltimore: Johns Hopkins University Press.

Further Reading

*Konstan ch. 5; *Moore 131–39; for prostitution sentimentalized, see Keuls, E. (1985) *The Reign of the Phallus. Sexual Politics in Ancient Athens*, Berkeley, Los Angeles, and London: University of California Press, 188-91.

∾ *3D Menaechmi 351–69*
Drop-dead Gorgeous: The Babe

Lust doesn't always rule the comedy roost. But it's usually in the mix, and ogling and gawping at/and pawing and groping keeps spectators and actors at it. In general, predatory desire scents "totty" or "hottie" regardless of social status or availability, sanctions or decorum. So whether they shimmy from the sidelines or turn into central players in the plot, the parts for females always have at least a margin for how to play the sexiness factor. Don't they?

Meter: mixed song (**p. 147**)

351–56

352/3   Understand, after the threefold imperative: *ut id **quod opus est fiat***.

356   **amanti amoenitas malo est, nobis lucro est** four dat., in two pairs of indicative objects plus "predicative" dat., "Loveliness is (for) a pain for a lover, (for) a gain for us."

In a trice and a flash, "Sexie" has told one servant *not* to close the door to her place, but to go back in and sort it; other staff, pl., still inside for her to boss, must fix the place for a lunchtime dinner-date, create the mood for love, nice and expensive. Instantly in charge, this smooth operator runs a classy joint, strings the guys along. That is, her guard is down. She has no idea what's about to go down: she's on the receiving end of the plot.

357–60

357   **aït** scans here as a double short dissyllable.

358   **qui mihi est usui** indicative object plus "predicative" dat., "who I have a use for"

359-60 **hinc ultro fit, ut meret, potissumus nostrae domi ut sit; |
        . . . alloquar ultro** lit. "from here [from where I'm standing] it happens more than readily, in accordance with what he's worth, that *chez moi* he's *numero uno*; . . . [so] I'll go talk with him" [equally] more than readily."

Yes, the door's wide open for the guy who's paying, because "he's worth it"; comedy's cooking up a treat in there. A telltale millisecond of uncertainty, and this babe thinks she knows where he's at, just because he comes into view; she doesn't say who he is, yet, but there again she's never known who he is (a man with a past; somebody's twin). She's about to strut her stuff, chat up a stranger, but both of them are going to be taken in: as they enter, she calls him by name—what we've been waiting for—and so dumbfounds him without realizing it. As the twins zigzag in and out of the play, their shared name sets them sharing each other's lives, not least their sex lives . . .

361–68

361   **animule mi** this sort of sweet-talk diminutive is called a "hypocoristic" (like *Erotion*), = "soul-ie," and when you m-m-mouth *mi, mi-hi mi-ra* make sure you mean it: this is the marvelous woman either twin would love to come home to.

>   **mira uidentur** English uses the sing., "it seems amazing":
>   where Latin can use pl., "things seem amazing" (followed by
>   acc. and infinitive).

362 **foris, fores** she turns on the charm, to turn on her chum: her
>   open *fores*, "door," shouldn't keep him *foris*, adv., "door-side,"
>   i.e., "outside"; nor should they be apart—as her words, and her
>   speaking them, should be acting out.

363 **quam** supply *patet*. This doll talks like a lady—such a polite
>   little "do come in" serenade: it's up to you to decide how much
>   leering you put into "this" here.

364 The gap in the manuscripts can't be helped—the improvised
>   metrical form of Plautus' ditties has stumped copyists and
>   editors (try: "la-la-la-ing" in appropriate falsetto here).

364-68 **omne paratum est ... neque ... est | ulla mora intus. | pran-
>   dium ... hic curatumst: ubi lubet, ire licet accubitum** in-
>   between the pers. verbs, the impers. constructions pay lip-ser-
>   vice to due deference even while the hustler gushes, "All's set
>   up ... there's no hold-up inside ... lunch is seen to here: when
>   it is your pleasure, it is in order to proceed to recline" (*ire ...
>   accubitum*: the supine after a verb "of motion" expresses pur-
>   pose). It *half*-doesn't matter who she's talking to ...

Such an open-hearted operator, this dream hostess with the
mostest. "Everything" on a plate—"ready, just the way you wanted,
when you wanted it, here, now, lunch is served, come get it, please be
seated," all tumbling out as she lays it on thick as you please. Comedy's babes are all about *lubet*, *licet*, and, one way and another, "lying
down"—until and unless they step out of the wallpaper, and burst
through the sex-objectification to take on "a life of their own."

Bibliography: See on **3B** (**p. 67**).

∾ 4 The Thick of It: Five of the Best

∾ 4A Truculentus 482–548
Outmaneuvered: The Soldier and The Whore

The Hooker and her Maid—go-between, assistante, and protégée—
here take over the theater. They skin all the males of all they've got,
finding every chink in their armor and nailing them dead. This
amazing sight, of a woman-on-top who stays there, makes for a
slam of a straight-from-the-shoulder plot, with no frills. You want
it crude—you got it. "Phronesium," or "Wisdomina," will unload all
three clients who show up today, making a special point of robbing
them blind "while they see it happen" (111), and she will end the play
by inviting in any spectators who are looking for a good time. In our
scene she squeezes her big-talking booby Soldier's surprise soft spot.
The pair of them—and baby makes three—are a perfect parody of
family—and the life their lives bar them from.

Meter: *trochaic septenarii* (**p. 147**)

482–98

482 **ne exspectetis . . . dum praedicem** "don't wait . . . until I proclaim"

483 **dvella** = *du-ella* "wars" (here disyllabic *dwella*, by "synizesis").
The form survived in formal citations and martial poetry;
unlike *bellum*, it kept the notion of "duality" in a "duel" up
front.

485 The acc. and infinitive construction continues, "that Homer-
son [a Greek acc., from nom. *-ides*] and a thousand (people)
thereafter can be recounted." With *pote*, "having the power,"
"able" (indecl. adj.), supply *esse*.

(487 is cut by editors as just too lame a variant on 486 for even the
lumbering soldier to get lumbered with.)

488   **non laudandust quoi plus credit qui audit** meaning to sound authoritative, the Soldier spouts clichés: the Latin gets taut by economizing on antecedents: supply *is* (1) with the gerundive *laudandus* + *est*, "(the person) is to be praised," as antecedent of *quoi*, indirect object of *credit*, and again (2) as subject of *credit*, as antecedent of *qui*, "whom the person who hears trusts/believes more."

489   **pluris est oculatus testis unus quam auriti decem** "An eyed witness is worth(y of) more [gen. "of value"] "than ten eared witnesses." Soldier coins a quotable "proverb," in which *oculatus* and *auritus* are folksy-jokey colloquialisms.

490   **non placet quem** the impers. verb is another bid for authority, "I am against the person whom..." *mussito* isn't usually transitive: the syntax is loose, "(while) the rank-and-file soldiers mutter."

494   **facile ... facunditatem** a facile conceit blurring the stems *facio, -ere* and *for, -ari* ("do" and "say"). The abstract noun (only here) is possibly the wordy warrior's invention, "Eloquenticity." The pun on *fecunditatem* passes him by.

495   **mihi habeam pro praefica** "may I treat so-far-as-I'm-concerned as a woman-in-charge (of a funeral)"

496   **eapse** f. of *i(s)-pse*, "herself"

497   **decumo mense post** "nine months afterwards" (adv.)

497-98   **ad amicam ... | uiso ... quid ea agat** "to my lover's *I go to visit-and-see* how she is" (trading on both ideas in *uiso*)

Yes we have been waiting ages for the long-promised fall-guy Soldier to come play true-to-form (see **Fig. 4**; cf. notes on **3A**). He doesn't disappoint, dishing out long-winded homilies on the reasons why we'll get no long-winded bragging from him, and so achieving his character type's usual blend of pretentious vanity and lame rhetoric after all. His attack on glib towny rhetoric and praise of raw Courage (*Virtus*) both echo favorite themes of sturdy Roman sermonizing (see especially Marius' "Unaccustomed to Public Speaking as I am" speech in Sallust, *Jugurthine War* 85 and satire from Lucilius, 1196–1208W; see **Further Reading**).

Fig. 4 Comic Soldier carrying his pack. A Hellenistic terracotta figurine.

Phronesium's scam is to borrow a baby and screw the supposed father for maintenance and anything else she can get out of her soldier, arriving back today from nine months of mercenary campaigning out East. We suddenly realize this is one way for a footloose Soldier to father the baby son he'd evidently give all he's got for, though he's obviously too thick as well as sold on his own virility to wonder if sex for sale is such a good environment for secure paternity. Never crosses his mind. (Unlike streetwise Ovid's, even as he is—momentarily—worried sick that his Corinna has put her life in jeopardy by aborting "their" child:

In getting the load of her pregnant womb dislodged
    Corinna lies exhausted, in peril of her life.
Heaved all this danger on herself, and kept it dark from me,
    so she's earned my rage—but rage subsides through fear.
And yet, she did conceive by me, or so I believe and trust.
    Not the first time that Ovid treats what may be true as fact.

Amores 2.13.1–6

Classic Roman comedy provided story-lines, situations, and catch-phrases for later writers of love elegy such as Ovid, where the *adulescens amator* monopolizes the "script," for adventures in the first person. Plautus is indispensable "background" for reading Latin love poetry, and for studying Roman erotic culture, gender, and domestic lives.

499–502

499   **uide quis loquitur** the verb is indicative not subjunctive in colloquial "parataxis," "take a look-see, who's talking?"

500   **tibi opus + est . . . ut** "there's a need for you to," "you need to"

501   "Would you, to whom I was up to this point so *bad* an advisoress [*mone-trix* may be a made-up word here], beat me in doing *bad*?"

502   **uin** = *uis-n(e) adeam* "do you want (that) I go to," "you want me to approach?" The unaccented ("enclitic") particle *n(e)* merges with the word that opens a question, and regularly loses metrical value, as here.

Madame has arranged an elaborate "bedroom scene" for this meeting at her doorway, dolled up in a special "new mother's" robe and languishing in suitably "blue" post-natal stress. The maid is sent to soften up the soppy new dad first. A good seven performers crowd the stage for this hoot of a scene.

503–12

503   **euge** "yeah!"

      eccam "See her there!" a feminine acc. "of exclamation"

      ecastor "sure, by Castor!" (an "expletive" used lots by women)

503-4 **salue . . . saluom te** — she was about to complete a polite greeting with *uolo*, lit. "be well . . . I wish you well," "Be well . . . hope you're well?"

505   **ecquid mei simile est** "is it in any respect [= "at all"] like me" (in comedy, *similis* always takes the gen.)

506   **qui-n(e) ubi natus** + **est** a combination of exclamation and interr. "Why! When he was born, . . .!? ."

507   **papae** "wow!"

      tvi = *tui*, pronounced as a monosyllable, "*twi*" (by "synizesis")

509   **erre** imperative, "off you go," "get away!"

      nu-dius-quintus (= *nunc dies quintus*) adj., "now-day-fifth," "four days ago"

510   **inter tot dies . . . aliquid actum oportuit** "in an interval of so many days, something must have been done" (impers. verb, with *esse* understood)

511   **quid illi ex utero exitio est** lit. "why is there for him an exiting from the womb"

One (more) thing the Soldier knows nothing whatever about is childbirth and babies. The big schmuck is also gibbering from sheer joy over his little trooper.

513–30A

515   **Mars . . . Nerienem** the Roman goddess Nerienis, wife of Mars, hardly figures in mythology; her name is Sabine for "Manhood/Courage," Roman *Virtus*.

      peregre adv., "(from) abroad"

516   **quom** in Latin of this period, "causal" *cum* clauses were often in the indicative, but here the temporal component is strong, lit. "now that you've come out successfully and have been increased with children . . ."

518   **qui me interfecisti . . . uita et lumine** lit. "you who have intercepted me from the light-of-life"; so *inter-ficio* is a common euphemism meaning "kill"

519-20 "and who have, through your pleasure, put into my body ["of," "partitive" gen., =] some great pain, through which malady I am still now in misery"

521   **heia** "oh!"

       ab re "away from [= "not in"] your interests"

523   **oppletis tritici opus** + **est granariis** "there is a need for you of (abl.) granaries filled with (gen.) corn"

524   **ne . . . hinc nos exstinxit fames** "in case hunger obliterates (has obliterated) us from here" (pf. subjunctive)

525   **sis** = *si uis*, "please" ("if you will," *uolo*)

526   **ego-met** a strengthened form of *ego*, "I myself"

       neque . . . queo = *et nequ-eo* (*neque eo*), "and I can't "

527   **mea sponte** abl., "with my volition," "voluntarily"

528   **pigeat** impers., "it would annoy"

529   **experiere** = *experieris* (deponent 2nd person sing. fut. indicative)

The reunion turns into an audience, as the bullish hulk runs into a wall of warnings to approach softly and on command. He must realize *she almost died*. He's allowed bedside, for one peck. Hey presto: now, after what she's done for him, he knows *he truly loves her*, and will prove it. With all he's worth, the fool. Obviously no one else exists outside his fantasy.

530B–35A

531   **his te dono** "I present you with these."

adduce hoc tu istas Stratophanes will bark orders at his servant to fetch out his captives—his presents—"to here" (*hoc* = *huc*).

531-32 **domi | svae** "at their home" (locative)

533 **paenitetne te** impers., "doesn't it make you regret"

534 **quin** = *qui-ne* (conj., "how/so that not," with subjunctive)

   examen super adducas "without you introducing a swarm on top (*super* = in addition)"

   quae mihi comedint cibum rel. clause "of purpose," "to eat up my food."

"A brace of princesses? What a liability!" Phronesium is the best household manageress ever. She may be play-acting here, but she really does make the perfect wife and mother—for herself.

535B–39A

535 **ce-do** imperative, "gimme"

537 **hocine** = *hoce* + *ne*, "Is this . . .?" The unaccented ("enclitic") particle *-ce* retains metrical value before the second particle *-ne*: so *hicine, haecine, hocine, hocine . . . dari*: acc. and infinitive "of exclamation," "(to think) that this so-tiny thing should be given me on account of so-mighty labors!"

538 **iam mi auro . . . constat** lit. "now stands for me at gold " (abl. "of price")

   contra "to my disadvantage"

539 **etiam nihili pendit** "she also weighs as worth nothing" (gen. "of value")

More exotic spoils all the way from Asia (Phrygia is where Troy once was). Mme does mean to "keep" the little number "for herself," but she's not finished yet.

539B–41

540   **tus . . . amomum** "incense of the sort called 'Blameless' in Greek" (i.e., of card-amom spice)

Third time unlucky, as the two mute extras in tiaras and chains, and their hyping, shrinks to one posh "red mini-dress," and now a bijou, itsy-witsy, perfume jar and a one-liner. Soldier is getting closer, and all this will do fine in terms of cash-convertible contribution to "labor costs," and to anticipated overheads; but next time round he'll have had to watch and learn it's cash she appreciates about a guy—and not just a "retainer" plus a "sweetener," but finally all the loot in his money-belt. By then, he'll be tortured by Phronesium's cruel display of preference for his rival from hicksville, who bids the contents of his neck-pouch before they both get taken in(side) for a good time.

542–48A

543-44   **uiginti minis | uenire** "be sold for [abl., "at a price of"] twenty minae."

         dono dedi "I gave for [as] a present."

546   **uerum** "but"

         num ne-uis "surely you don't not-want me" (with acc. and infinitive)

547   **quo** "to the place where"

         cubitum uenero "I'll have come to lie down/have sex" (supine with a verb "of motion" to express purpose). He's not thinking about dinner.

Soldier reverts to the way he wants "today" to go—a party off with the lads followed by return for a night in the bed he's paid for (not out of keeping with standard arrangements, e.g., Propertius 1.3). As if she'll have got over herself by then, and the newborn baby makes no difference.

548B

548 **quid illuc noui est?** "what's this new development?" (lit. "what of something new is that?" gen. "of respect")

Soldier sticks around instead. To watch the positive reception of the third customer's train of gifts—party-fare—and shoo it away. He'll never have an inkling about the play he's in. As for Phronesium, the baby she borrowed will be returned to its real parents, and get them wed, and the father (namely this third "lover") will remain her true friend (especially 388), and renew their liaison when he needs a refuge from marriage, as he will, and misses her, as he will (879–82). These two never deceived each other about the dynamics of their "sexploitation" deal, and their affection sticks out a mile between brutish Soldier and callow country-boy.

Recommended Edition

Enk, P. J. (1952–53) *Plauti Truculentus*, 1–2, Leiden: Brill is an *editio maior*, in Latin. Use Nixon, P. (1916) *Plautus*, 5, Loeb Classical Library, Cambridge, MA: Harvard University Press.

Translation

Tatum, J. (1983) *Plautus' Darker Comedies*. Baltimore: Johns Hopkins University Press; Tatum, J., in D. R. Slavitt and Palmer Bovie, eds. (1995) *Plautus, The Comedies*, 2, Baltimore: Johns Hopkins University Press.

Further Reading

*Duncan 147–52; *Konstan ch. 8; *Moore ch. 8; Dessen, C. (1977) "Plautus' satyric comedy: the *Truculentus*," *Philological Quarterly* 56: 145–68. On Plautus' women, see *Rei, *Dutsch, and Johnston on *Poen* (**2B**) ch. 5. For Lucilius' *Virtus* fragment, see E. H. Warmington, ed. (1967)[2] *Remains of Old Latin*, vol. 3: 390–92.

◆ *4B Casina 780–854*

Invitation to a Wedding: Comedy Gets Married

The old man wants to recharge the batteries? His Mrs keeps him straight by exploiting her privilege, to dress the bride indoors. As the wedding train heads across stage, and into the house next door, we know the women have been into the costume cupboard, and "Here comes the bride—with a beard!" It's burlesque season, always the time for a drag queen, and *Someone's* in for a shock . . . (See **Fig. 5**.)

Meter: mixed meters; *song*, including 798–99, 801–7, 809–14, *trochaic septenarii*; 780–97, 847–54, *senarii* (**pp. 146–47**)

Fig. 5   The heart and soul of the modern British panto(mime), the Dame and the Principal Boy. Families take their families each Christmas time.

780–87

780   **si sapitis** "If you [pl. = the women] have any sense"

tamen "all the same, though, . . . ," anticipating the "but I shan't be with you" of the next line.

781   **ruri cenauero** "I'll be having dinner [fut. pf.] in the country" (locative)

783   **rus prosequi** "to escort to the country" (acc. "of motion towards")

784   **facite uostro animo uolup** "treat your selves pleasurably," "have fun"

786   **tandem** worn out with the waiting, "*finally*"

luci abl., "by day" ("in the light")

The man-of-the-house gives up on mere food, and will take over the reins as soon as the wedding party crosses into public, male, space—for his night out, having "first enjoyment" of the family's young female slave Casina (perhaps fragrant as the spice *casia*, "cinnamon" [cf. 225, and 812 below], but also punning both with "Girl from Casinum, a town near Rome"—and with *casa*, "house", as in "[Little Whore]house"?). His cunning plan was to marry her off to his country-estate minder, slave Olympio, who gets lucky when a lottery is arranged to decide between Olympio on one tag team, and his wife's candidate for groom, her town slave Chalinus, on the other side. Together, the wife-next-door (Myrrhina, "Myrrhdah"), her feline maid Pardalisca ("Pantherina"), and this wife Cleustrata ("Glory-of-the-Army") make a formidable trio, pulling all the strings behind the scenes. They pass unobserved by both cast and us "through the back gardens" (613), and they string out the cooking in the kitchen. Now they surrender, passing the bride across to meet her groom next door; but stooge and superannuated stud haven't seen Chalinus around for quite some time now . . .

788–92

788   **quod futurum** understand *esse*

790 **ego eo quo me ipsa misit** "I'm going (to) where Herself sent me"

792 **tu hic cunctas** "you dawdle here." The verb is generally deponent.

Round One to the women: no home cooking today for the alpha male. That's all the maid popped out to rub in—oh, and to fool us into thinking the guys' wait was over now, when it isn't. Now for tonight's "oats." Pardalisca will pop back in a trice.

793–97

793 **si uis** "please"

794 **dicere hic quiduis licet** "it's ok to say anything-you-like here"

795 **si esurit, nullum esurit** "If a lover is hungry, still he's not at all *hungry* (for *food*)." *nullum*, adv. = *nihil*.

797 **meus socius, compar, commaritus, uilicus** "my ally, mate, fellow-husband, estates manager." The big-build cue for entry—spot which term of camaraderie is specially dreamed up for this very moment!

The groom comes to collect and escort his bride, out front, from her old home to her new life. As the Prologue stressed, "slave marriages" were unRoman, though they happened, he insisted, in South Italy (Apulia) and Carthage, as well as in Greece (67–74). But that can't stop us wondering if there are any concessions to Roman custom in the comedy's send-up ceremony: on at least one pattern in Greek culture, a "best man" escorted the happy couple on a carriage between the two family homes, after the feast at her parents', and everyone joined in with the wedding chant to send them off on their way. A Roman groom left first to await his bride at home, while young boys carrying torches led her there and everybody made plenty of lusty noise (see G. Williams in **Further Reading**).

798–808

799   "make the whole town square buzz with my wedding song"

800   **hymen hymenaee, o hymen** suitably age-old mumbo-jumbo, unRoman-sounding whoops, for the ritual, "wedding god, wedding song, o wedding god."

801   **quid agis** "how you doin'?"

    mea salus . . . haud salubriter "my well-being/my salvation" puns with "not being well/*un*saved."

    adeo "besides"

    at ego hercle nili facio "well I, by Hercules [= "gawd!"], rate it as nothing" (gen. "of value")

804   **remorantur remeligines** sing-song frustration in this complaint, lit. "hold-ups hold me back"

805   **procedit minus** impers., "it progresses less"

806   **quid si etiam suffundam hymenaeum, si qui citius prodeant?** "what if I also fill up the wedding song/flood the place with wedding song, to see if somehow (*qui* abl.) they step out quicker?"

807   **censeo** "I reckon so," "I agree"

Starving and sex-starved groom and best man will skip the wedding feast, and start the wedding song, to see if that winkles or flushes the bride out into their clutches.

809–14A

809-10   **dirumpi cantando . . .; | illo morbo, quo dirumpi cupio, non est copiae** lit. "to burst with singing . . .; there's no opportunity ("partitive" gen.) to burst through that malady I crave to burst through." He's double-punning (see on 841) to get exploding lust into the limelight.

811   **ne** interjection, "yes indeed." Naturalized Greek (*nē* or *nai*), this has *nothing* to do with the negative conj. *ne*.

812   **nimis tenax es** "you're too [= so] hang-on-'n'-never-let-go"

num me expertu's (= *expertus es*) **uspiam?** "you haven't tried me somewhere, have you?" Take it that twitting and dogging the lecherous old goat should mean you load every jibe with innuendo, involving more-or-less indiscriminate sex, buggery, bestiality . . .

813 **di melius faciant** lit. "may the gods make it better."

ex-itur impers., lit. "there is a coming out"

Excitement in frustrated loins and minds produces randy "horse-play" between the "boys," as the "travesty" looms: this is the perfect opportunity to think, maybe salivate, about the roles of cross-dressing in comic theater tradition, such as vaudeville or pantomime (see Gold in **Further Reading**). The extraordinary fetishization of the "virgin bride," dolled up in bright yellow (our white) and paraded past the assembled community through the streets to meet her "maker," marks the most intense insistence on gender bifurcation just at the critical moment when all the members of two entire clans and their satellites changed their mutual relationships, and the ripple-effect spread clean across the township. No wonder there has been so much talk down the years of "sacrificial" attributes and/or function for The Bride. And no less speculation on the liaison between humor and men-in-drag. *Cas* reeks of it, all through.

814B–28

814B **iam oboluit Casinus** "the scent has already got to someone—the scent of Casina, but in the masculine gender." This remark has to come from someone who knows this bride's not female, and someone not above joining in with grubby talk about sexual attraction, and stink (or scent, if you will). It must be Pink Pardalisca who comes out with it on her way back in, before cracking on with her big number.

815+816 **super attolle limen pedes** "over, lift, the threshold, your feet" must be a ritualistic touch of doubling up the required action in word-order.

817-21 **uti . . .** a naughty inversion of wedding-day prayers for lifelong subordination of bride to husband, hamming up the sonority and repetitiousness of solemn formulae.

822 **uir te uestiat, tu uirum despolies** "let him keep you in clothes—and you'll strip him to the bone."

823 **noctuque et diu** "by night and by day."

ut uiro subdola sis "that you should be a-bit-cunning for your husband" (dat. "of disadvantage")

825 **malo maxumo svo** understand "(she'll be that) at the cost of big big bad to herself" (abl.)

ilico, | ubi tantillum peccassit "on the spot, when she's lapsed this-little-much" (the "*s*-form" pf. subjunctive)

826 **mala malae male monstrat** "the bad girl shows (to) a bad girl badly"

828 **id quaerunt uolunt, haec ut infecta faciant** "they seek-want this—to make all this unmade." Jamming the two verbs together is more over-cooked indignation, amplified by the "figura etymologica" in *-fect- . . . faci-*.

Spot what sounds right and what rings wrong in this bridesmaid's blessing: for a start, she hexes the carrying over the threshold for good luck by making it mark departure, not arrival at her new home—*before* she bids her "*start* this journey into eternity" (817–18). The "rite of passage" goes right off-course, sounding the right sort of notes but singing for gynocracy: "all power to you (over *him*)," "victory over virility to the victori-ess," and "her words, her command, shall prevail" (819–20). She must do it for womankind—and, lo and behold, the men are trapped into giving her a head start, by refusing to interrupt and so rise to the women's bait—and forfeit the wedding night.

829–34

832-33 **amabo** fut. indicative, "I'll love ya," i.e., [the Roman women's word for] "please."

integrae atque imperitae huic | impercito "*unto* her be spar-
ing [*-ito* is a polite imperative, originally a 3rd person form]
*unt*ouched and *unt*ried (as she is)" (dat.). The alliteration underwrites the wish, as if the concepts all come from the same
stable, and belong together. They do *now*.

The matron-of-honor formally delivers bride to groom, calm
and dignified as can and should be. Now the women must leave the
girl to fend for herself—"go easy on a virgin out of contact with all
previous experience." *This* touch, and its sentiment, surely hits the
spot. It's the telling pause between the jousting and the leering we've
been hitting on, and the release ahead when the pawing and bruising retaliation camp it up, and take it away. With nuptials to end all.
Now the women have brought their showpiece out into the open,
they have usurped control of "public space" for the showdown: it's
the men's fault, intent on dominating the bedroom interior, only to
over-achieve, and find only horny hairy smelly scary androgenic
pheromones (see Andrews in **Further Reading**).

835–43A

835   **ne time** "have no fear"

       euax "yippee!"

836   **pol** "by Pollux!" (everywhere in Roman chat)

837   **meum corculum, melculum, uerculum** this lecherous inton-
       ing of pet-names hums through "mine heartlet" and "honey-
       let" before making up "springlet" to make three.

       heus "hey!"

838   **malo . . . cauebis** "you'll keep away from the bad" (the verb
       usually takes *a*(*b*) and abl.)

840   **immo** "no, rather"

841   **huius quom copiam mihi dedisti** "now/since you've given me
       a chance for/sexual access to [with gen.] this person"

842   **corpusculum malacum** it's the other lech slavering this time,
       "body-let *douce*" ("soft," in Greek)

843   **uxorcula** "wifelet," a colloquialism rarely attested

The predators lock horns as they slurp over the quarry, and can't wait another moment before making grabs for the flesh.

843B–48A

845-46   **institit plantam | quasi luca bos** "she has stood her foot (sole) on (mine) like a heffalump" (The Romans called elephants some strange sort of "cow," with stories to "explain" it.)

847   **aeque atque huius** "equally as hers" (i.e., "as much as hers")

848A   **papillam bellulam** more sonic drooling from the lips, setting up more to come, "what a beaut boobie" (acc. "of exclamation"). But this jumbo Cinderella is a toe-cruncher.

848B–53

848B   **ei misero mihi** "oh no, alas for poor me" (dat.)

849   **non cubito, uerum ariete** "not with a forearm, but with a (battering-)ram," and with a groan joke on its way:

851   **at mihi, qui belle hanc tracto, non bellum facit** "but from me, who handle her *beautifully*, she doesn't take *booty*" (lit. "make war on," with dat.). Told you it was coming: boom.

852   **uah** "aha!"

       quid negoti est? "what's the hassle?" ("defining" gen.)

       ut ualentula est exclamation, "How fit-let she is!" Another dumb "hypocoristic" (a diminutive form for a term of [mock-] endearment), and they're still not done. Do groan. We're supposed to.

853   **paene exposiuit cubito. cubitum ergo ire uolt** "she almost laid me out with" that "forearm," so that our mutt of a comic genius can pun, "that's because she wants some foreplay" (supine with a verb "of motion," *cubo*, to express purpose, "to go to bed"). Boom, boom.

And Goldilocks has a killer forearm smash. She promises to be quite a handful between the sheets.

854

854   **quin imus ergo?** "why aren't we off, then?"

i, belle belliatula one last time, "come beautifully beautif-let!" One last gaga sound-bite of lust out loud, and that made-up specially for here, to boot.

In fact Snow White promises to be a she-ila and a half! The bodily and verbal mauling that starts here will come to a climax when man and wife and best man get to grips for the bedroom farce. We'll *hear*, along with the crowing womenfolk, all about the fumbling and fondling and finding and freaking, first from traumatized Olympio, then from his boss, pursued on-stage by the civil partner he left halfway to paradise . . . And we'll be back for the finale, in **5B**.

Recommended Edition

MacCary, W. T., and M. M. Willcock (1976) *Plautus*: Casina, Cambridge: Cambridge University Press.

Translation

Tatum, J. (1983) *Plautus' Darker Comedies*. Baltimore: Johns Hopkins University Press; Beacham, R., in D. R. Slavitt and Palmer Bovie, eds. (1995) *Plautus, The Comedies*, 1, Baltimore: Johns Hopkins University Press; Christenson, D. (2008) *Plautus: Casina, Amphitryo, Captivi, Pseudolus*, Newburyport, MA: Focus Classical Library.

Further Reading

*McCarthy ch. 3; *Moore ch. 9; *Slater ch. 5; O'Bryhim, S. (1989) "The originality of Plautus' *Casina*," *American Journal of Philology* 110: 81–103; Williams, B. (1993) "Games people play: metatheater as performance criticism in Plautus' *Casina*," *Ramus* 22: 33–59. On the dirty old man: Cody, J. M. (1976) "The *senex amator* in Plautus' *Casina*," *Hermes* 104: 453–76. For our scene, see Gold, B. K. (1998) "«Vested interests» in Plautus' *Casina*: cross-dressing in Roman comedy," *Helios* 25: 17–29; Williams, G. (1958) "Some aspects of Roman marriage ceremonies," *Journal of Roman Studies* 48: 16–24; Andrews, N. E. (2004) "The semantics of space in Plautus' *Casina*," *Mnemosyne* 57: 445–64, especially 459–63.

ᖄ *4C Asinaria 746–809*
The Foolproof Contract: Scriptwriting Onstage

It's always annoying when they make you watch someone read or write something on paper during a play. It challenges any troupe to squeeze drama, action, *fun*, out of it. It gets very close indeed to asking you why you're sitting there in the theater, rather than wait till the *Reader* comes out, when you can sit and enjoy the writing for what it is . . . In this passage, Plautus gives his answer, showing why it's worth the hold-up on stage—to make fun of writing, with all its pretensions to fix things, tell the world what's to happen, and what not (see **Further Reading**). In this scene of spoken, unaccompanied, verse of legalese ped*antics*, a pair of bit-part "villains," the second loverboy and his smarmy slickster of a pal, try to draw up rules of non-engagement, in an attempt to buy out The Girl's services. A perfect antidote to Ovid's "Sex Manual," which trains young dudes for singles combat:

Here it's ok for you to say lots, of cryptic chat-up
    in code, and she'll realize what's being said to her;
and to write, in full, featherlight sex-talk in faint wine
    so she can read on the table *she's your queen*;
and to gaze into her eyes with eyes confessing the flame
    —without a sound a look can take on speech, and words.
Do see you're first to grab each glass her lips have touched,
    and the bit the girl drinks from, see that's where you drink.

And any sort of food she's sampled with her fingers,

> you go for it, and as you do, there's a touch of her hand for you.

Plus, wish and wish you impress the babe's guy

> —he'll be more use to you once you've made him your friend.

Over to him, should you draw lots to swig, cede first go,

> to him, present the used crown discarded from your head . . .

If you have a voice, sing. Balletic arms?—Dance.

> And any gift you can impress with—go impress.

Getting drunk for real's no good; faking it will go down well.

> Do see your sneaky tongue trips up and lisps and lisps out loud,

so anything you do or say that's red-blooded to excess,

> let the reason—"too much wine" is what it is—be believed.

And wish her majesty luck, and good luck to the guy she sleeps with

> —but wish bad luck for her guy, in thought, without a sound.

Then, when the table's cleared and each partygoer leaves,

> the throng will hand you the chance to get up close to her.

Inject yourself in the throng and mosey right up to her gently as she goes.

> Twitch her tail with your fingers and play footsie, toe to toe.

Now's the time, for talk with her. Hicksville Modesty, beat it,

> outahere. Maybe Fortune favours the brave—but so does Venus.

Ars Amatoria 1.569–82, 595–608

Ovid has already posted "cruising dinner parties," on his way to getting to women through the maid and smuggling in the love-letter (229–48; 437–86). Once he reached this scene, before leaving for bedtime, he's been recycling one of his own first adventures as an instantly expert novice at playing "comic loverboy," *Amores* 1.4. Now he's turning all the lads of Augustus' Rome into Ovid clones! Our passage is included in Murgatroyd, P. (1982) *Ovid with Love: Selections from* Ars Amatoria *I and II*, Wauconda, IL: Bolchazy-Carducci, 349–72. I give *my* account of the sex manual, "In Ovid with bed," in Gibson, R., S. Green, and A. R. Sharrock, eds. (2007) *The Art of Love: Bimillennial Essays on Ovid's* Ars Amatoria *and* Remedia Amoris, Oxford: Oxford University Press, 77–95.

So, here's how (not) to program a customized-executive reserved-exclusive living doll. Here's how to stop a play in its tracks, so you can groan some more. Loud.

Meter: *senarii* (**p. 146**)

746–50

746   **age-dum** imperative, "come on now"

    conscripsti the contracted pf. form (for *conscripsisti*)

    syngraphum "contract," a Greek term for something Romans could all deplore but were tied to, up to here

747   **leges pellege** the jingle ties the ideas tight, "read-the-regs" (*lex* was etymologized from *lego*.)

748   **poeta es prorsus ad eam rem unicus** "you're straight up [*pro-uorsus*] the one-and-only poet for this job."

749-50   **faxo** "I'll make sure" is a colloquial fut. indicative, used parenthetically.

    lena, leges . . . translege now tie in prostitution to prose: "red-light mama—read-the-regs." (The verb is found only here.)

750   **audi(s)n(e)?** "You hear?"

"Show" us, so we can "hear-hear-hear" (746, 749–50). Some build-up for this "poet" among lawyers. The contract with us is for "a reading"—where we listen and they speak and act out the words.

751–55

751-52   **Clearetae | lenae dedit dono argenti uiginti minas** "had given as [dat., "for"] a gift twenty minae of silver/cash to Mme. Clearete"

753-54   **noctes et dies | hunc annum totum** acc. "of duration," twice in a row, for the row of "24/7/52" (in *our* calendar)

    quiquam abl., "anyone"

755   **scribas uide** understand *ut*, "you see you write"

The point is made right away, and then stands for the duration: the co-signatory is "reading" critically, listening hard; he could intervene at any moment, on any detail. We should play too, and shadow him. If it's that good (or that bad) a contract, it surely can't go on leaving elementary loopholes like this one lurking in the detail. But, please, not too much more of this—these "saving clauses," pride of the clerical machine, are pure mind-rot, no? To a T. Every dotty jot.

756–73

757   **quod . . . nominet** the first item in a long and dull, dull, dull, procession of "legal clauses" citing and re-citing scenarios aptly begins with the proper name, "as to . . . her naming . . ." (*quod* with subjunctive).

760   **in foribus scribat** "writing on her door" seems a crazy way to warn off "other men," but it does add a layer to this script about writing writing.

763-67 more layers of written paranoia, writing to proscribe scribble: "no incoming mail, no mail in the house, no wax-tablets (*ceratus*: adj., "waxed") and no "no-good paintings" (i.e., pornographic tableaux that don't pull it off?) to source wax for writing a letter/the alphabet (*litterae*).

764-65 **ni in quadri-duo | abalienarit** "if she hasn't got rid ["transferred to another's ownership"] in the four-day period . . ." (*quadri-dies*)

765   **quo abs te argentum acceperit** ". . . from which [i.e., "from when"] she received the cash from you"

766   **tuos arbitratus sit, comburas** "it shall be yours to adjudicate whether you'll incinerate" (indirect question; understand -*ne* with the verb)

769   **ad eorum . . . quem** "to any of them," picking up the pl. latent in *conuiuam neminem*

770   **aspexit** fut. pf. indicative, or pf. subjunctive (= *aspexerit*)

771   **tecum una** "together with you"

pocla "goblets" (= pl. of *poculum*)

potitet "guzzle"

772-73 The control freak must run the flow of booze, filling her up, letting her do the toasting (*propino*), but doing the drinking himself—only, somehow, so as to keep in sync, as they both lose their wits. Complicated business, this bingeing.

772 **ted** = *te*, here abl.; so, too, early Latin retains *med* for acc. or abl.

It's a winner: *satis placet* (773). Control traffic through her door, on hind legs or on paper?—check. Get the party going?—so far so good.

774–91

774 **segreget** "let her remove"

775 "and no squashing any person's foot with her foot": see the lengths that rigorous attempts to robotize someone are bound to lead to. Talk about neurotic!

776 There must always be a "next couch" at a dinner-party to worry about, and people are going to need a hand to get up or down through the evening.

778 And the harm in handing round rings for a look? Isn't it obvious? Well?

779 No pressing the dice on some other guy (*tali*: "ankle-bones," used for dicing). Now the attention falls on speech some more— and on naming names, not hiding behind shifty prons.

781-83 So to prayers to the gods—make that to goddesses only ("let her call upon any goddess she likes" [*sibi . . . lubebit*: "it will please her"] to be "favorable to her" [*sibi . . . propitiam*]); and if there's any question of "being afflicted by a god" (*religiosus*: here anything from some voodoo or curse—clap, say, or menstruation—to a headache, to a girl thing, anyhow none of our guy's business), he'll do the praying. Mustn't go trusting girls to gods unmediated.

784   Not forgetting paralinguistic communication: for who needs
        words, written or spoken? Ancient prayers *could* be silent,
        and—leaving the gods aside—humans have developed an en-
        tire lexicon for tiny visual gestures that mean so much (*nutet,
        nictet, adnuat*: "nod vigorously, blink-or-wink, nod yes").

785-86 **ne quid sui membri commoueat quicquam** lit. "and she
        shan't stir any(thing of a) limb of hers at all" (*ne quid*, adv.).
        Bodies send messages, not just heads and faces. But a human
        deprived of movement is still going to send out messages—
        not necessarily the ones you want. The nightmarish negativ-
        ity reaches a logical limit of anti-life absurdity here.

786   **optume est** "(that) is in the best way," "very good"

787   **sci-licet** "for sure" (= *scire licet*, lit. "one can know")

788   **deme istuc** "remove that."

        equidem "I (for my part)." One thing you can't legislate against
        is legislation that over-achieves. Talk about painting yourself
        into a corner.

789   "I do *not* want her to have a case, and say she was told not to"
        (supply *esse*).

790   **captiones** "tricks," "quibbles"

        uerum "true" (supply *est*)

791   **quid ni?** "why not?"

        Take the party slowly, one phase of play at a time—but never lose
        sight of the objective: the right "bedroom" action. Never forget that
        any legal document demands 360^0 reading—from all parties' point
        of view. What ammunition, what aces, might it already be handing
        the hire-ess? Control suddenly seems paper-thin, and the writ of
        reading-culture is in tatters.

792–802

792   **perplexabile** "ultra-enigmatic" (only found here). Back to lan-
        guage monitoring, and the twin impossibilities of eradicat-
        ing hidden meaning in your own tongue, and of covering all

known languages; then on to the mouth—tongue, lips—and oral-erotic symbolism, simulation, and stimulation; from *lingua*, 793 to *linguam*, 795!

794   **forte si tussire occepsit** "if perhaps she's begun to cough" (an "*s*-form" pf. subjunctive)

795   **proserat** "stick forward (= out)."

796   **simulet, quasi grauedo profluat** "mime snot pouring out" (lit. "mime as if snot's pouring out")

797   **hoc ne sic faciat: tu labellum abstergeas** "let her not make like *this*; (instead,) *you* do the wiping (off)." Here, in *hoc* and *sic*, is confirmation of 794, *ne sic tussiat* ("let her cough like this— *not*"), that we'll have been right if we have been making sure that one or preferably both of them, draughtsman and investor, have been rising to the challenge: how to make the ruled-*out* scenes come alive in the course of their recital, yet be cancelled in the act? In themselves, "sexy" tongue-wiggling and lip-swiping are a challenge, when served up with fake spluttering cough and mock streaming nose; harder to do the girl *not* getting to see to herself, but instead having herself seen to by her controller, which must call for split-second timing from the double-act.

798   If her face *isn't* wiped by Diabolus, he risks her giving someone a kiss "in full public view" (*palam*). This would be a "hand kiss" thrown, "like *so*," from fingers-to-mouth away toward an admirer? It would be—that's to say, it would be acted out despite, but in tandem with, its denial—if *I* were directing.

799   That melo*dramatic non*-gesture concludes the banned entertainment for the party girl. Now for her manager and madame: "mother."

800   **nec ulli uerbo male dicat. si dixerit** "and she'll not abuse anyone" (*ulli* dat.) "*with* a (= one) word." (abl.) "If she does . . ."

801   **haec multa ei esto** "let this be her fine/forfeit."

801-2 **uino | ut careat** that she do without wine" (abl.)

802   **scitum syngraphum** "(what) a clever contract" (acc. "of exclamation")

Back on track, this pen is bang on the money: *pulchre scripsti* (802). It's also gotten physical, slithering down the slippery slope to sordid images of the sex-kitten hacking and snotting and smearing, while her ma is refused the booze and badmouthing she lives for. If this is the girl playing dirty sexy money for all she's worth, still drying out "mother" brings onto the radar an arid world without pleasure. In a trice, we'll find, such a combination of gynephobic spite and hate is the reason, the reason why paradise lost.

803-7

803-5 **coronas, serta, unguenta** "crowns, garlands, oils." As the imaginary *non*-party closes down, the hireling is pictured sending off what must be a standard set of offerings to fetch to the temple of Love, namely the makings for another party, and maybe heading for, not Venus, but some dreamboat Cupid. "Your slave" is to "watch" where her slave takes the presents—are they for "a man"? The deal is to monopolize the "Pretty Woman," but that plants and propagates, projects then proliferates, spectres of promiscuity in every object, and any action. Funny, really.

805 **Venerine . . . an uiro** "whether . . . to Venus or to a guy". (*eas* scans as a monosyllable)

806-7 "If perhaps she says she wants to stay clean" (*pure . . . habere*), then let her give in return as many filthy nights as she stayed clean." Now it's late, very late, into the night, and there's only one thing left to pin down. The ultimate phobia on the agenda is the prospect of 365 nights with a "Living Doll," nights spent obsessing over all the ones with no sex.

This has got to be funny: men and women at odds over which of them finds or wants sex dirty? Ditto, periods? And personal hygiene? At the same time, there's the investor who hears the clock ticking, and his cup's always half empty. The one surefire thing we know about "guaranteed satisfaction" is that it is guaranteed to self-destruct; at least, it is in comedy, where all automatism is the enemy.

808–9

808 **nugae** "trifles," "rubbish." "No, this is no funeral" (*mortualia*: "death-rites," "funeral lamentation," a rare word).

809 **profecto** "for-a-fact"

Give comedy carte blanche to write "love for money" into a sure-fire recipe, and that's what you get—a "rubbishy death-march" in, and about, denial. The sketch lifts right out of the play, in which this lover-boy has shown up with credit card and contract just too late on. He and his stooge have written a script to beat all, but they're just about to catch their rival's Father at it, partying away at Madame's joint, *with* both the son *and* the floozie. He's buying one night of fun for himself, as his cut of the year of togetherness he's managed to purchase for them. Our dynamic duo will at once fetch in the beloathed Wife-and-Mother to catch him at it, and hound him back home in disgrace, the senile delinquent. So they play "snitches," and are here to attract the boos.

Recommended Edition

Henderson, J. ed. (2006) *Plautus* Asinaria: *The One About the Asses*, Madison, WI: Wisconsin University Press.

Translation

Henderson, as above.

Further Reading

*Konstan ch. 2, *Slater ch. 4. On our passage: James, S. L. (2006) "A courtesan's choreography: female liberty and male anxiety at the Roman dinner party," in C. A. Faraone and L. K. McClure eds. (2006) *Prostitutes and Courtesans in the Ancient World*, Madison, WI: University of Wisconsin Press, 224–51. More on this and other documents read (out) on stage in Scafuro, A. C. (2003–4) "The rigmarole of the parasite's contract for a prostitute in «*Asinaria*»: legal documents in Plautus and his predecessors," *Leeds International Classical Studies* 3.4; and Sharrock on *Pseud*, **3A**.

∾ 4D Rudens 938–1044
The Tug of War: Finders and Keepers

Here Plautus goes mushy on us ("ah!"). In this exotic thriller, we travel to a distant land, of seas and sand—and . . . storm . . . and . . . strand . . . The pay-off is like winning the lottery: fished up in a net is a trunk, and in the trunk is a box, and in that box are the keys to one Happy Ending. I shall rope in the main lines of the plot at the end of the notes, but here, when and where you least could expect it, comes a daughter's salvation. For there dangles her future, with everyone else's, at the end of a cord. Everyone loves *The Rope*, with its expert play between unravelling tension and secure expectation. It has all the serenity of escapist melodrama you could ever ask for, and works every time, whether you are the Director of the Shakespeare's Globe Theatre, London, putting on your own outrageously awful adaptation for your swan-song (2005's *The Storm* produced by The Tempest Company; the script available in print as *Storm: or The Howler: an Appalling Mistranslation by Peter Oswald of a Roman Comedy by Plautus*, Oberon Books: London, 2002), or you're a bunch of classical students putting the original across for all it's worth (see **Fig. 6**).

Meter: mixed meters, including **938–44**, *iambic octonarii*; **945–46**, *iambic septenarii*; **963–1044**, *trochaic septenarii* (**pp. 146–47**)

938–44

938   **hanc . . . rudentem complico** "I wind up this rope" (*rudens* is to all appearances a pres. pple., meaning "braying," so "a screamer").

939   **mitte modo** "just let go."

   bonis quod bene fit haud perit "a favor to someone good isn't wasted" (lit. "what is done well for good people does not die"). Pompous, pious, and pushy preachifying.

941   **nil habeo . . . piscium** "I have no(thing of) fishes" ("partitive" gen.).

ne tu mihi esse postules "(so) don't think that I have" (lit. "that there is (to me)").

942   **uuidum rete, sine squamoso pecu** "a sopping wet net, with no scaly herd." The first phrase is humdrum, the second the height of poetic flamboyance.

943   **non . . . quam tvi sermonis sum indigens** supply *tam . . .* , "not (so much) . . . as I am needing a chat with you." *tvi* is monosyllabic, "*twi*" (by "synizesis").

944   **odio** "with disgust."

Gripus has just finished his solo song of whooping joy at his lucky catch, and starts to haul away the net and its contents; but Trachalio arrives to hold him back, and means to reel him in on the rope attached to the net. Their tug of war starts with these ultra-lengthy lines that stall the action (from *mane* to *mane*). We're cued to observe, not the "nothing" Gripus points us to "see"—the *lack* of sea-food—but the symbolic "complexity" of the play's principal prop, *the rope*. Ropes are ties; they catch people and property; the catch, and double-bind, is

Fig. 6   The tug of war scene from the *Rudens* put on by the St. Olaf College, Northfield, Minnesota, with improvised English riffing on original Latin. Production by James May, music and lyrics by Anne Groton, 2003.

that they are for taking away but they are also for holding tight, drag-
ging back again, then tying down, and even tying up. Their workings
lend themselves to emphatically "cinematic" theater, where we watch
marvelous—supernatural—puppetry pulling invisible strings to net
the entire cast, scenery, and script, and magically unpack the contents of one nested vessel after, and inside, another, until not one loose
end is left. Lo and behold! Very likely, "Gripus" is *both* the Greek for
a "Catch (of fish)-*cum*-Basket (for fish)," *and* a riddling pun with the
Greek *for* "Riddle." When his catch, the omni-capacious trunk and
then the rush basket, or casket, inside, are "opened," *Rud* is set fair for
"solving" its impasse, in a "dénouement" to beat all (from *de-nodare*,
"un-knot"; *solue uidulum . . .* , *solutust*, 1142–43, *res soluta est*, 1412;
you can find "unhitching a rope" is *exsoluere restim*, at 367 . . .).

945–53

945   **caue . . . malo** "you'll keep away from the bad."

   quid tu, malum, nam me retrahis? "what are you (at), you
   pain (lit. "bad"), here, you tugging me back?" *nam* starts off
   an annoyed query.

946   **at pol qui audies post** "well, lord, how (*qui*, abl.) you'll listen
   later!"

   quin loquere quid uis "why not—*say* (imperative) what you
   want?"

947   **eho manedum** "hey, wait a mo'!"

   est operae pretium "it is worth the effort" (lit. "there is a reward of the effort [as to the thing . . .]").

948   **prope nos** "near us" (prep. + acc.)

949   **ecquid est quod mea referat?** "is there anything that concerns me/my interests? (*re-fert* = abl. of *res* plus *fero*, intransitive verb (often impers.), with *mea* or *tua*).

As the verse rhythms chop and change, the actors up the tension:
the bristling Gripus realizes he is not just being stopped in his tracks,
but actively "winched back" (*retrahis*): he is still being told to "wait"

(*manedum*), even after he has "retreated" to telling Trachalio to speak his mind; we know he's taken the bait when he starts asking for more talk, and he goes like a lamb when issued with terms for being trusted with the low-down: while information-wise they are no farther forward from one *audi* to the other *audi* in this passage, a note of confidentiality, and even conspiratorial tete-à-tete, has been sounded, and Gripus has got *interested* in listening—in fact, *self*-interested.

954–62

956 **no(ue)ram dominum, id quoi fiebat** "I knew the owner to whom that happened."

959 **indicium domino non faciam** "I won't shop him to [lit. "I won't make a pointing to"] the owner."

960 **quid inde aequom est dari mihi? immo hercle etiam amplius** "what is fair to be given from it to me? No, lord, still more."

961 **domino dicundum** supply *esse* (acc. and infinitive), "it must be told [gerund] to the owner."

In this miniature imaginary "consultation," a case-study from Trachalio "comics up" the whole burden of the *Rud*, as Gripus is tricked into agreeing, hypothetically, on "terms" (*condicionem*) for "fair play" (*aequom*) which would make the slaves partners in crime as accomplices after the fact: for in *their* case, "witnessing" a find *meant* informing (to) a master, since slaves could not own property. Gripus will be invited to apply this blackmail to his own look-out right now; but we will see how this foundling play's hypothesis is that "lost property" should be traced to rightful ownership, until *everyone* realizes there are strings attached to all relationships, in any world where belongings belong. Identity theft will prove a trap that catches the thieves; delivery on longings for long-lost family ties will see fair play for the family slaves, too, with longed-for liberation from being property to having their own share in society. Here, playing away in all-at-sea exile from normality, utopia tells its far-fetched parable, salvaging human flotsam and jetsam right before our very eyes: and "all of it relates to *you*" (962).

963–70

963   **uidulum istum quoius + est noui ego hominem** "THAT
      TRUNK, I know the man whose (trunk) it is." A blaring
      mixed-up doubled acc.

964   **quo pacto** = "on what terms," "how"

      inuentust = *inuentus est*

966   **nihilo . . . pluris . . . quam quanti** gen. "of value," "not more
      . . . than the amount that" (lit. "of more worth by nothing . . .
      than of how much worth . . .").

968   **ne te speres potis** understand *esse*, "don't hope that you are
      capable."

969   **dominus huic, ne frustra sis, | nisi ego nemo natus + est** "to
      stop you wasting your time, nobody has been born [= "there's
      no one on earth who is"] owner to this."

"That trunk-you-got-there" is hooked out of its subordinate
clause so that it presides over the mood-shift to the steady meter that
will last clean through the rest of the dialogue, and its identification
is underscored as the stage "property" to which this mellow drama
is devoted. Insistent triple repetition tracks and trails the comedy's
metaphor of "slave-owning" to stand for all varieties of "belonging
to" (*dominus . . . dominus . . . dominus*, "master/owner"; *quoiust . . .
quoius est . . . quoius fuit*). The tussling slaves themselves belong to
the same system as that trunk. Just in case you don't see the catch,
they're not the only ones.

971–86

971-72 **ecquem . . . piscem meum? | quos** "any fish of mine? | (Fish*es*)
        that . . ."

973   **manu asseruntur** "are claimed by hand" (i.e., as property, es-
       pecially a slave).

974   **habeo pro meis uenalibus** "I treat/regard as my items up for
       sale."

975   **certo** adv., "certainly," "for sure."

976   **qui minus hunc communem quaeso mi esse oportet uidu-
      lum?** "how, I ask, ought this trunk to be less shared-in-com-
      mon for me?"

978   **quippe quom extemplo in macellum pisces prolati sient** "in-
      deed, as soon as the fish would have been brought out into the
      fish-market."

980   **nemo emat, svam quisque partem piscium poscant sibi** "no
      one would buy, each of them would demand their own por-
      tion for themselves" (*quisque* regularly takes a pl. verb).

982   **ausus + es etiam** "have you even had the nerve?"

983   **in manu non est mea** i.e., "it's not in my control."

985   **nacti sunt** from *nanciscor*, deponent, "they acquired"
      meum potissumum est "is especially (n. as adv.) mine"

986   **siquidem quod uas excepisti** "if indeed you've caught a(ny)
      container"

Our all-too-convincingly "shameless" parody lawyers dangle
market forces and maritime lore on the end of their lines of argument
(*impudenter impudens*; *impudens*): no one owns the stocks in the
sea, which belongs to all "in common," *so* fishermen own what they
catch; but why this "so"? Why does it stop being "common property,"
something to share and share alike, when it's caught? And, equally,
how can a piece of property taken from the sea count the same as fish
that belong in the sea? Because fishing nets whatever the hook-and-
line "pulls out." *Excepting* a, or any, man-made vessel . . . Life and
its system of distinctions and discriminations seem more elemental
and less clearcut away in Africa and exile, more like the ocean than
a land. Will the principles that ought to underlie protocols come out
in the wash? (See *Konstan in **Further Reading**.)

987–1000

988   **uidulum piscem** introducing, that newly discovered species,
      "the trunk fish"!

989   **non occupabis omnis quaestus** "you *shan't* seize all the liveli-
          hoods."

990   **et uitorem et piscatorem te esse . . . postulas** "you claim you
          are both basket-maker and fisherman."

991-92 **uel . . . uel** "either . . . or"

          ne feras "don't pick up/take away"

993   **scelus** "wickedness" (used as an insult)

996   **nil agis, dare uerba speras mihi te posse** "you're getting no-
          where, you hope you can fool me" (lit. "give me words").

          furci-fer "fork-carrier" ("slave punished by wearing the arm-
          stretcher," used as an insult)

997   **quo colore est, hoc colore capiuntur pauxilluli** lit. "with
          the color it has, with this color they're caught (when they're)
          teeny-weeny."

998   **sunt alii puniceo corio, magni item** "there are others with
          red skin, likewise big."

999   **in uidulum te bis conuortes** "you'll turn yourself into a trunk
          twice over." First a beating will turn the skin red; then it goes
          black(-and-blue).

1000   **denuo** "from new" (= *de nouo*)

Sarcasm ridicules the assimilation of trunk to fish, with a showcase dilemma: "*either* (A) show us the "trunk-fish" *or* (B) don't run
off with non-fish from the sea." Which provokes specialist claim to
privileged expertise rare as any counsel's; and just as forthcoming,
too: "a rare and shy visitor, comes in this suit as a minnow, or full-
grown in red or black varieties . . ." Now, comically enough, tropi-
cal seas do nowadays sport many "trunkfish" species, of the genus
Ostraciidae, but Plautus' case in point is that (A) these claimants are
"talking the talk," trying like the creators of law to find words that
"bamboozle," i.e., inventing legality through inventing reality (*dare
uerba*; cf. 1071), and (B) the imagination is liable to morph into any
reality it creates. For that trunkfish is already turning, before your

very eyes, just as a slave's skin goes first red, then black, into the very image of its inventor. The play consists in a whole chain of linked cases of identities packed *into containers*: that is how images work.

1001–11

1003 **salue, Thales** "howdy, Einstein!" A legendary Greek egghead/ brainiac.

1004 **nisi das sequestrem aut arbitrum** "unless you appoint a third-party (to hold disputed property pending settlement) or a third-party (to decide the dispute)"

1005 **sanun** = *sanus* + *ne*.

1006 **helleborosus** "manic" ("full-of-hellebore")

  cerritus "crazy"

  amittam " I'll let go"

1007 **in cerebro colaphos abstrudam tuo** "I'll shove punches away in your brain!"

1008-9 **te . . . exurgebo quicquid umoris tibi est** double acc., "I'll squeeze out you, whatever liquid you got!"

1010 **affligam ad terram te** "I'll smash you to the ground!"

  piscem . . . polypum "an octopus." It seems to be an "etymology-conscious" phrase (rather than another daft fish species), explaining why the Greek loan-word is adjectival, meaning "multi-pede."

1011 **quin tu potius** "why not rather . . . ," here with an imperative

Yes, this word-mongering is our play for today (*uerba facimus, it dies*). We've been shown that the key to these people's future is locked up in the trunk, coded into what the trunk holds, but also what it means. Now we must find someone to decide who gets it, i.e., who gets what. This someone is to get it all, *and get it all*. He will preside, and help magic fair shares into pure serendipity. To resolve the case, a third-party ombudsman is needed, and, truly, the trunk *shall* decide—silly, or crazy, or not. But before Gripus can let go his grip, and cut *Rud* some slack, we step back a little, for some more knockabout threats to orderly procedure: from mad-house to rough-house, the swapped insults go marine, limbering up for a showdown: sponge vs. octopus.

1012-18

1012   **nisi malum frunisci nil potes, ne postules** "you can have the pleasure of [acc.] nothing but bad (trouble), don't demand it/ count on it."

1013   **at ego hinc offlectam nauem, ne quo abeas** "I'll turn my ship to face you from here, so that you don't go away anywhere."

1014   **proreta isti naui es** "you're look-out for that ship" ("prow-man").

       gubernator "the one steering" ("helmsman")

1015   **omitte** "let go, drop"

1016   **ramenta fies fortunatior** you'll become luckier/richer by a scrap."

1017   **non probare . . . mihi potes** "you can't make-it-right for me."

1018   **aut ad arbitrum reditur aut sequestro ponitur** impers., "either it's going back to an arbitrator or it's being shifted to a deposit" (i.e., "put in trust").

Here verbal stunts give way to balletics: Gripus is off? No, Gripus isn't going anywhere. As both man their boats, Trachalio outmaneuvers the angler nautically, heading him off before coming about (*hinc* vs. *hinc*). The result is the same (*mane*), and the lines of engagement are no different (*mitte rudentem; mittam: omitte uidulum,* 1015: *non amittam; ni . . . amittis,* 1006, 1009). But that star tightrope has come back into its own, for another twist and turn, as the pair steam round and have at each other, pitching net vs. arcing rope (like gladiators). There's plenty of mileage here for acting out the dogfight. When Trachalio repeats his demand for a third party solution—or else goes back to extorting "a share" (*pars*, 1017 = 973), he gets us back to *discussion*, back to case law, and his opening gambit.

1019–28

1019 **quemne . . . ?** "(a trunk) that I . . . ?"

1020 **mea opera, labore et rete et horia?** "through my effort-'n'-toil, plus net plus fishing-boat"

1021-22 "Am I who watched you get hold of this from afar any way less a thief than you, if the owner whose it is should come now?"

1022 **nihilo** "by nothing (less)," "not a bit"

      mastigia "(slave) always on the wrong end of a whip"

1023 **et** "and (yet)"

      facdum ex te sciam "you just make sure [-*dum*] I know from you" (understand *ut*)

1025 **nisi quia** "except that"

1028 **nec tu me quoiquam indicassis** "and don't you inform on me to anyone" (an "*s*-form" pres. subjunctive).

1029 **tu taceto, ego mussitabo** "you keep quiet [-*eto* is that polite imperative, originally a 3rd person form] and I'll keep a-mumbling" (-*ito*, an "intensive," or "frequentative," verb formed from *musso*).

The stalemate holds (*mane* vs. *abire*), as (A) Trachalio threatens "informing" on "theft" to "owner/master" (*dominus quoiust; fur . . . socius . . . et fur . . . nec fur nec socius sies; nec tu me quoiquam indicassis* = especially 956–59). Trachalio steals the role of interrogator (again), but he has relapsed into his smooth-talking lawyer persona some more, and hands the fisherman his chance to take them all the way back, right back, to where Trachalio came in: so (B) native wit finds the answer—cut the knot, stop talking, no more "chat" (*sermo*, 943), "go their separate ways." As they say: bother, end of (= problem solved/crisis over). *That* is "fair play" (*aequissimum* = *aequom*, 960). See how it takes the hick slave of witty ("urbane") comedy (A) to object to the unspoken law of "city law" ("urbane law"), namely that it knows no place for nobodies such as he (*nescio, neque ego istas uostras leges urbanas scio*); and (B) to perform in his parody version of "law unto himself" the definition of law as self-interested declaration of "what belongs to whom, and what not" (*hunc meum esse dico*: blocked, met, and affirmed by Trachalio: *et ego item esse aio meum*; cf. 1071, 1230): since a slave had—owned—no voice before the law, he could only escape into and through silence, and make his silent escape. Our escapist farce, though, will make him glad he does get tricked, into "letting go," finally (when *he* will be "let go," "manumitted," "set free" (*emittat manu*, 1388, 1410). You could sum up and hold up (this) comedy as mirror to society—the place where, as the pimp prompts, "It's up to me to arbitrate whatever my tongue swears to" (1355, *meus arbitratust, lingua quod iuret mea*).

1030–44

1030   **ecquid condicionis audes ferre?** "are you prepared/willing to fetch an(ything of an) offer?"

1032   **refero condicionem** "I make an offer back (a counter-offer)."

te . . . aufer modo "(No,) just off *yourself* off!" Abuse deals in crude puns this way (*ferre-refero-aufer*), the worse the better.

1033   **oportet uicinos meos** supply *no(ui)sse*, "I should know my neighbors."

1034   **ubi . . . hic** "where(abouts round) here"

porro illic longe usque in campis ultumis "far away (over) there, in the distance, the whole way off on the last plains there are"

1035   **uin** = *uis* + *ne*

1037   **fiat** "so be it, ok."

1038   **intra praesepis meas** "inside my pen"

1039   **abiudicabit ab suo triobolum** "he'll award-to-someone-else [*ab*-, "away"] a three-obol [a dime] from his own."

1040   **ne** yes indeed"

1041   **quamquam istuc esse ius meum certo scio** "though I know for sure that this is mine (by right)"

1042   **nunc places** "now you get my support"

1043-44 quamquam ad ignotum arbitrum me appellis, si adhibebit fidem, | etsi ignotust, notus: si non, notus ignotissumust lit. "though you are driving me to an arbitrator I-don't-know, if he applies good faith, | even if he's someone-I-don't-know, he's someone-I-know: if not, (as) someone-I-know he's the-someone-I-don't knowest (of all)." This is where we came in: gruff fisherman trumped (*quamquam . . . , quamquam . . .*) by clever-clever wordplay from the lover-boy's faithful slave. They're *both* salt of the earth—this is Plautus' *Rud*, not one of his usual romps.

Trachalio's still posing the questions; Gripus now wants *him* to "get away" (*abeas*, as just came to him, 1027). Neither is changing his tune (*rudentem amittis*; *mane*), but their altercation now shifts back to swapping terms and counter-terms (*condicionem*, 957), and a winning proposal for an ombudsman: at once "slackening the tension," and letting Plautus "save the day"—and give over stringing us along (*remitte restem*; *salva res est*). Once Gripus' master-and-owner Daemones is chosen to sort out fair play, everything *will* be delivered in "good faith" (*fidem*, as at 955): *he* will fix terms—with that other "rightful owner-and-master," his opposite number, the pimp (*uin condicionem . . . ferre me?* ~ *condicio placet*, 1407, 1417). And yet, he'll comment for our benefit; Gripus has heard it all before, in some comedy or other, when his master starts nobly/naively preachifying on the theme of the baited nets of life waiting to ensnare unprincipled greed, "O Gripus, Gripus . . . ," and knows the audience clapped but left it behind in the theater once the play was over! (1235–48 vs. 1249–53).

The gods hauled back the faithless thieving pimp's get-away with a storm that wrecked both his ship and Daemones' home in exile. In the ship were the pimp and his crony, with Daemones' long-lost, kidnapped and enslaved daughter, and her friend and fellow-sex slave. The girls cast off the rope that tied their dinghy-let to the ship (367), and, "hooray," as if (in)visibly piloted (165–66), reached the beach ahead of the "washed-out, cleaned-out," villains (537, 579–80). Ashore, the storm blew the tiles clean off the roof: the household will be restored this blessed day (see especially 152–53). The temple and priestess of Venus next door meanwhile shelters—"mothers" (289, 410)—the girls, who get (fresh) water drawn for them at Daemones', filling the sacred urn stamped as "property of Venus" (458–84), *just like them*, "the spitting image of Venus" (421). When the pimp drags the girls from sanctuary at the goddess's statue inside, they take refuge at her altar out on stage. Thanks to Daemones' house-slaves and Trachalio, they are saved from further tugging off to their fate worse than death (especially 780), and when Gripus' catch arrives for Daemones to adjudicate, the pimp has already been taken off "into jail" (715, cf. 498, 872, 876, 889), for cheating Trachalio's master, the play's "Prince Charming," of the down-payment he'd handed him for the girl. Taken off, that is, at the end of "a rope round his neck" (853, 868, *obtorto collo*— the slave punishment which gives "Trachalio" his name in Greek—"Neck[t]ie").

Thanks to Daemones' commitment to fair play, the girl will get to list the symbolic toy-tokens as they are lifted from the opened trunk, linked on a neck-chain, verified for the benefit of both cast and audience by a triumphantly ostentatious ritual parade, Unpacking the Trunk. Where (A) in the earlier interlude we heard the local fishermen rattle off a string of mouth-watering riches from the sea (297–99), while "venerating Venery" (305), and (C) later on we will inspect the villains' share of the trunk's contents—a fortune in gold coins in a purse together with silver in a neck-pouch, plus all the vessels and containers needed for a party (1313–14, 1318–19)—while their owners itemize them, so (B) next we'll focus on the fetishized tokens of the girl-daughter-bride-to-be's identity (1081, 1153, *crepundia*, "rattlers"), her "parents locked up" in a casket woven from rushes (1144, 1147), fished from inside the trunk inside the ship in the sea (especially 389). These are: a sword inscribed with father's name, Daemones, and a double-axe engraved with mother's name; a tiny silver sickle and a pair of clasped hands, plus a toy *windlass*; and the gold amulet given her by father on her birth day—now re-bestowed on this her *re-birth* day (1156–59, 1169–71).

Now the comic chorusline of fishermen had included "shells" in the catch they prayed for (297, *conchas*, 304, *concharum*), and specifically dubbed themselves "marine thieves and shellites" (310, *conchitae*); when Trachalio prayed to Venus to protect the lovely girls at her altar, he reasoned that Venus was born from a shell, so she should not neglect "these girls' 'shells'," punning comically but irresistibly on their genitals (slang, *harum conchas*, 704). So see how everything fits when Daemones orders the thanksgiving party, with "lambs and pigs for sacrifice" (*porci sacres*, 1208). Because in the crunch comic touch of symbolic decoding of the daughter's precious trinkets, Gripus' comic gripe had punned unmercifully on that "windlass" (*sucula*, also "sow-let"), telling her "Why don't you go straight to hell, with your windlass/sow-let and with your piglets," where "piglet" *also* slanged outrageously on the girls' genitals (*porculus*, 1170).

Ultimately, then, the storm that relentlessly reeled in and towed back "home" ship and dinghy, purse and pouch, casket and trinkets, villains and girls, thereby fetched Venus her holiday party, fished from the sea in net and rope to deliver a daughter into the sanctuary of marriage; Trachalio's good faith is rewarded with freedom and the other sexy girl for a bride; Gripus (still in chagrin wishing himself *swinging* at the end of a rope, 1415, cf. 1189) is credited with a sum large enough to buy him freedom out of the reward due his master-owner Daemones, for recovery of the pimp's treasure; and the pimp gets the rest of his cash back, plus a bonus of forgiveness and even a share in the celebratory party. The divine Prologue had promised on behalf of *this* play "I am just the way you see" (3), and so it proved, too, for all those with eyes to see: nets, lines, ropes, rushes—and every one of them another "windlass" roping in the catch of the season—at once "shell" and "piglet." Signed, sealed, and delivered, too, as comedy's boxes of tricks give up their prize contents to view.

Recommended Edition

Fay, H. C. (1969) *T. Macci Plauti Rudens*, Bristol: Bristol Classical Press; or Sonnenschein, E. A. (1901) *Plautus* Rudens (*editio minor*), Oxford: Oxford University Press.

Translation

Smith, P. L. (1991) *Plautus. Three Comedies*, Cornell University Press: Ithaca; Watling, E. F. (1975) *Plautus*, The Rope *and Other Plays*, Penguin: Harmondsworth.

Further Reading

*Konstan ch. 4; Leach, E. W. (1974) "Plautus' *Rudens*: Venus born from a shell," *Texas Studies in Literature and Language* 15: 915–31. For the play's band of fishermen, see Lowe on the "chorus" of *Poen*, **2B**.

∾ *4E Amphitruo 361–462*
The Slave Meets His Match: Identity Theft

Our passage presents just one segment from what is deservedly the longest scene in all Roman comedy, playing on the many strategies that this society used in order to deny its servants full Human Personhood and Individuality, and generating energy and direction from mockery, menace, and destabilization of those precious fictions: without procedures for establishing and authenticating personal identity, there could be no such thing as society, or persons; only chaos. Send-up an "S.O.S." Or two.

We should already guess that Sosia (Greek for "Savior-ino/Survivor-ist") is blazing a trail of humiliation for his master, and look forward to King Amphitryo taking a bow later in the play. You're not going to believe this, but the story (everyone at Rome knew it) is that Amphitryo King of Thebes is returning tonight in triumph from a nine-month campaign in faraway Greece; Jupiter King of the Gods has simultaneously inspired the victories and, while Amphitryo has been away, impersonated him in order to sleep with the unsuspecting Queen Alcmena, while his son Mercury guards the door.

So Amphitryo too will run into himself, on his own threshold, in the person of Almighty Jupiter, *his* impersonator. As anti-hero and clown slave to wily wheeler-dealer junior god, so master and head of household (*paterfamilias*) to the supreme deity . . . No wonder this mold-breaking script began by announcing that it would merge comedy with tragedy, to make a first ever, hybrid, "tragicomedy" (51–63). Here is Jupiter, the deity who grants Rome victory over all real foes, trading Theban triumph over stage enemies in Greece for a naughty comic lover's access to a wife's bed. And here is Alcmena, who would only ever sleep with her husband, yet she is miraculously due to deliver twin sons, before "tonight's" crazy caper is over. One baby for Amphitryo, naturally; and one (conceived this very night!) for his adulterous double, Jupiter—namely, Hercules, favorite hero of the now world-conquering Roman legions. When the boys come home, there are always secrets, scandals, and aspersions; and in Rome there was one helluva fun party all over town, too, including farce on stage.

You see, Plautus once paraded this play in Rome as itself "spoils" won from defeated Greece, and it still serves as a vehicle for celebrating Roman superpower, as it did at its first performance, courtesy of some magistrate's sponsorship, at a state festival in Jupiter's favored capital city (most likely to celebrate one more victory). It is a comic idea that this classical version of a "gospel" story should fit this comic theater like a glove; but that makes it upbeat, not irreligious—cult myth put before the people in carnival mode. When Sosia just practiced his messenger speech,—"lies, all lies," Mercury knows, as god, as god of lies, as the Sosia-in-the-sky—his story of victory at the front jazzed up every Roman general's glowing report back to the senate in Rome. (Julius Caesar would later write up *his* "account," *commentarii*, as *The Gallic War*.) And Sosia matched—satirized—the high poetry that was gilding these campaigns in epic verse, too, as they happened (especially Ennius' *Annales*, the national poem of the Roman Republic, but lost to us). Yes, this *A-m-ph-i-t-r-u-o* serves up comedy's contribution to the burgeoning culture of Roman t-r-i-u-m-ph. And comes out fighting (203–61). For once this domestic comic—tragicomic—theater has no problem in addressing public themes of superpower, finding ways to coax gunboat diplomacy on stage.

This exchange of words, reinforced by bouts of pantomime blows from Mercury, hands the god all the questions and robs Sosia of all the answers. Sosia's claims to know who he is are taken over by his Doppelgänger (his demonic double), one by one—until he faces demotion from slave status to non-existence. (For another double, see **3D.**) As for the god, in order to appear on the comic stage, he must take one of the comic parts—and play not just a slave, a trickster like himself, but for the sake of the scene, a muscular and belligerent doorkeeper, only too keen to bully his host self and reduce him to pulp. Between the pair of him, Sosia and "Sosia" amass a monster part of five hundred lines, over half the play, of foreplay.

Meter: *trochaic septenarii* (**pp. 146–47**)

361–65

361   **tun** = *tu* + *-n(e)* "do you . . .?" The word-order vigorously underwrites indignation: "You insist on keeping me away from home on my arrival from abroad?" (You—me; keep away—arrive; (from) home—from abroad").

362   **haecine** = *haece* + *ne*: "is this . . .?"

        domust = *domus* + *est*

        ita inquam Latin had no one word for "yes," but instead spelled out assent, as here, or dissent.

363   **praefectust** = *praefectus est*: "he is put in charge over (lit. "he is made in front of"").

365   **pro-gnatum** "sired by" (with abl.; past pple. of a high-style "defective" verb). Paternity and paternoster are the stock-in-trade of this jumped-up cosmic rigmarole.

Sosia's challenge to the stranger who blocks his homecoming sums up the encounter to come. The play's expected braggart, conman, and "Brains" is going to boggle, wrongfooted, at a loss, and be made to play straight man to the uncanny lookalike, and soundalike, only more so, in his path. A production should pack "Me and my shadow" by-play into the routine just the way the Marx Brothers would choreograph it (see the hilarious mirror-scene in their *Duck Soup* (1933), dir. McCarey, L.: search YouTube for "Marx Brothers mirror scene"). Mercury begins from definition of the slave in terms of the household he is attached to, i.e., its, and his, owner: master has been away on campaign, leaving his wife behind in charge, inside, and Sosia bears a message for *her*. But before he can get on with getting in, Mercury takes his name, eliciting a boast that is way too big for the slave's boots—as if he can own a free citizen's claim to filiation (on the "Marcus, Lucius' son" model: *M., L. f.*). At 365, Sosia abuses the aristocratic lexicon while he's at it—"scion of . . . ," indeed!—by juxtaposing it with ". . . Davus," a stock designation for slaves, ethnic in origin, rather than a proper "(proper) name." As these chanted lines of meaty verse proceed to accommodate rapid-fire repartee, you'll find Mercury generally takes over lines that Sosia began, thinking they were *his*.

366–77

366 **ne** interjection, "yes indeed"

tu istic "you, yes you, there," pron.

malo tvo "predicative" dat., "for/bringing about something bad for you"

compositis mendaciis abl. absolute, "having put together lies beforehand"

367 **audaciai** the archaic 1st declension gen. sing. termination adds a stilted touch of extra sarcasm (*au-dac-i-a-i*) to the mock-hype phrase, as if hitting the heights of hype.

consutis dolis a second abl. absolute synonymous with the first, added without connective (in "asyndeton"), to mark the introduction of colloquial imagery of craftwork with textiles for "crafty" plotting.

370   **uapula** colloquial Latin starred this appalling verb, act. in
       form but "pass." in sense, "I am beaten" (of a slave). As if the
       victim was the agent responsible for inflicting the torture,
       making masters hurt them.

371   **non edepol uolo ~ at pol . . . ingratiis** "I damn don't want (to
       be beaten) ~ Well, (get beaten) darn involuntarily," as if Sosia
       said "I don't want a 'For-a-Fact'," so Mercury can come back
       with "Well, an *in*voluntary 'For-a-Fact', then." The words need
       hamming up with mock "haymaking" blows from the god, as
       he goes on to spell out his witticism in 372.

373   **tvam fidem** an appeal to honesty, honor, good name regularly
       involved invoking the gods, whether in oath or as witnesses
       (*ob-secro*, "implore," brings in "the sacred"). Sosia doesn't
       know he's asking a god for mercy—the god, precisely, of di-
       plomacy, protector of messengers like Sosia, and of cheating,
       Sosia's speciality (as in plotting and scheming, acting and im-
       personating . . .).

374   **perii** . . . feel Mercury's words picking up poor Sosia's *plosive*
       (*p*-) to accompany his peppering and pounding: *par-* . . . *prae-*
       . . . *prae-*. (*prae-ut* is treated metrically as if two words, with
       elision of *-ae-*)

375   **fecisti** we must supply the object *me*, and understand that
       those bruiser fists have rubbed Sosia out of his own sentence,
       and out of existence.

376   **pro fidem** this is the interjection, "yea!" with acc., "in the
       name of."

       carnu-fex "butcher" or "executioner" (slang) is a frequent
       term of abuse in Plautus—but specially apt here, faced with
       "(flesh-)slicing fists" (377).

       The god is spurred to retaliate with comic aggression—in the
form of over-the-top abuse phrased in a hammed-up version of the
highest linguistic register ("ridgepole of ye daredevilrie"). Fittingly,
the two characters joust over their role of "Cunning Slave." As one,

each aims to land the sucker punch, when Sosia takes the bait offered by Mercury's inviting substitution of "scripted lies" at verse-end with "woven wiles." He tries a sucker pun, "woven tunic, yes—wiles, no"; but his other half then stitches him up a treat by seizing on "another fib"—and on the whole scene's master-term, "homecoming"—to crank out the killer groan joke: "Ha! Gotcha! You never came in a tunic, you came in a taxi" (lit. "on foot"). How galling to be so out-witted by . . . your self!

Worse to come, never fear (370–72). The bickering turns to bick-ering about the bickering. Sosia's cool put-down "That a fact?" gets the retort "Take that for lying—now that's a fact!"; and his feint, "Not for me thanks—that's a fact!" is just asking for "Free of charge—and that's a fact!" followed up without pause by a "No returns" move that sinks our "Clever Dick" by bouncing his flip phrase back at him: "*This* 'That's a fact' is a dead cert—it sure ain't optional!" Checkmate.

At 373–74, Sosia is taking a right pounding, and surrenders, beg-ging for mercy before the gods. He faces extinction, the occupational hazard of the comic slave; but that is the logical outcome if his claim to be himself gets him erased, because his adversary *is*, as he says, that self. Now, Mercury stops calling him a liar, because what he just said is going to be truer than he meant: "I've had it" will mark the moment he really "was a gonner." Now (375) Mercury's onslaught cows Sosia, he makes him sing: no, not master's slave but master's slave's slave—so "Sosia's slave," then—because talking under duress sure *ain't* optional: he's been taken over, commandeered, lock stock and barrel. "Those fists!" Appealing to the "citizens of Thebes" is Sosia getting above his station again (376).

378–87

378-79   **istoc magis, | quia** "more by (reason of) that fact that" (abl. of
         cause).

379   **uaniloquo's** = *uani-loquos es*

382   **qui** = *quis*, "who"

         uocare "are you called"

383   **peccaueram** "I tripped up" (colloquial plupf. blurring into pf.,
        as often)

384   **ne** "yes indeed"

387   **esse** supply *te* with *esse*, "whom you said *you* are."

At 380, Sosia's "muttered" aside plays with the idea that there are
plusses in not having to be Sosia. For a start, you could join in with
giving him a pasting and a licking. But "the gods" are unlikely to
grant his prayer, even if they can hear it! So far, though, he only surrenders both parts of his "handle" for his bully to choose him an
owner and name *ad lib.* (381 and 382).

Next he reaches for a killer pun to get him off the hook (383–84):
what he *did* claim out loud was to be "Amphitryo's Sosia"; but this
must've been a slip of the tongue, for "Amphitryo's associate" (*socius*).
All talk in bilingual Rome, along with its book culture and all international dialogue, risked Graeco-Roman homophony, voluntary and
otherwise, at every turn. We could say this is where Latin humor
was, if not born, then misconceived; and comic scripts *always* look
for verbal banana skins where slick acting *nearly* (but never quite)
passes itself off as pseudo-improvisational bungling.

This specimen is an atrocious flop—for both vowel length and
consonantal value. So . . .—so when Mercury pretends to *accept* it,
as if there *might* be a slave in the house called *Sŏcius*, but never more
than one named *Sōsia*, he *could* be dissing it as any kind of joke;
maybe more of a *mistake*, after all, from this so*sia*-called "Cunning
Slave." This repeats at once, when Mercury's turn of phrase, *fugit
te ratio*, meaning "(yes,) you blipped," but *implying* "your mind de-
serted you, you lost it there, you had one of your turns," and *saying*, "literally," "your reasoning *ran from* you," turns into a hook for
Sosia's latest dumb-insolent rejoinder, again phrased as a wish-and-
a-prayer, "If only your fists had done that," i.e., "had *run from* you
(and/or from me)" (386). Again the double lets this bit of banter by
reflex pass, resuming his own claim to own the identity (385, *esse . . .
Sosiam* ~ 373; 387, *ego sum* ~ 374, 379; cf. 381, *quis tibi erust* ~ 362): a
new move is signalled.

388–400

388   **ut ne** conj. = *ne*, so that not (with subjunctive)

390   **quando** "since"

        pugnis "in the fist department" (abl. "of respect"; but also "instrumental," "with" those "fists").

391   **fide** dat.

        meae "yes," we would say

394   **denuo** = *de nouo*, adv., "afresh," "again" (lit. "from new")

397   **ut-ut** indefinite conj., "howsoever" (with indicative)

398-99 **quin** "how not" = "so that not"

400   **med** = *me*, acc.

(401   This line is deleted by most editors, as certainly awkward metrically, and possibly intrusive rhetorically.)

In the "far-cry" epic tale of Amphitryo's subjugation of the Teleboans, an offer of "peace and freedom from disturbance" was communicated through envoys, but on non-negotiable terms amounting to capitulation; glorious victory was secured by the enemy's heroic scorn for dishonor, and sealed by the survivors' unconditional surrender, at the discretion of their conquerors. As so many horrified Greek and Greek-speaking states and coalitions were still finding out when their turn came to be faced or forced down by their world's greatest fighting machine, this *was* diplomacy Roman-style (see the Greek historian of conquest by Rome, Polybius, *Histories* especially 24.8–13). Now, when *un*heroic Sosia wants a peace treaty to sign—so that talks can be held—he is handed the temporary half-measure of a "truce," plus a pledge of good faith backed by a weasel-worded sanction—but this is then directly countermanded by immediate volte face (*ut ne uapulem* through *non nocebo* to *uapula,* 388, 391–395). It's the Greekling slave's own fault for supposing for a moment that "saying what you want to say" has a chance in the teeth of "force majeure" (*quid uis loqui*, 390 = 393, cf. 391 vs. 390, cf. *quando pugnis plus uales* = 396). All he does by appealing for "peace talks about talks" is invoke the gods again (*obsecro*, 388 = 373), so he can walk into the Roman god's imprecation, and make it come true: Sosia *does* make sure Mercury's wrath falls upon him. Not least by extorting the oath through distrust of the trickster . . . god, Mercury.

Yet the worm now turns, after the momentary breather, to allow the two Sosias to draw closer together (398 ~ 399–400), and release a spot of full-on mimicry, now the fisticuffs have overdone their darnedest.

402–15

403   **malum** "hell!" here an interjection rather than an insult aimed at another

404   **ex portu Persico** this is a suitably tantalizing detail that we can't securely assign to fantasy or to fact.

408   **malae** "jaws"

411   **ementitu's** = *e-mentitus es* "you lied all the way, thoroughly"

414   **ui pugnando cepimus** "we took by fighting with force [abl. of gerund, with "instrumental" abl.], we stormed," an official Roman formula in reports and citations of shock-and-awe.

415   It was, however, so rare for a Roman commander to kill the enemy chief that there were supposed to have been just three instances ever (see Propertius 4.10).

The duet/duel starts by sharing a line, swapping the same accusation of insanity, tit-for-tat (cf. 386). But then Sosia breaks away to talk with his idea of his self, checking over his consecutive memories of tonight's narrative that has brought him to this point, right from leaving the ship in port through to . . . the bruising he got from the human he thinks stands in front of him (*hic homo*, 407). His self-quizzing leads to corroborating evidence—the lantern he holds, the ache in his jaws; and his voice sounds reassuringly like him as the words come out—nothing like a dream sequence. His final—eighth and ninth—questions in the sequence are meant as resolution, threatening to banish "uncertainty" and exit the protracted scene of obstruction, "dithering" here on the threshold of home (*quid igitur ego dubito?* 409).

But his other self picks him up on the wording: "Why not go into *our* house?" ~ "What, *your* house?" 409–10). And the self-interrogation that tried to un-person, and so wish away, the hulk standing opposite by refusing to address him (407–8) has, (un)naturally, handed the interlocutor an opening to trump: Mercury begins where Sosia just started, leaving the ship in port (412 ~ 404), and then works backwards to hook into the epic war narrative as rehearsed by Sosia before he ran into his evil twin (especially 414–15 ~ 191, 217–18, 252)—though not before he overheard, and corroborated the truth of the story, unseen in the supposed darkness of the wings (247–49). Hence the surreal fun of prefacing this take-off to the life by falsely denouncing the original's "lies" (411). For once, that liar had told the truth, even though he did lie about it, too (197): as we shall soon see (423–31).

Right now, we've reached the stage where Sosia "doesn't (can't) believe, or trust, Sosia when Sosia hears Sosia tell Sosia Sosia's tale of Sosia's tale" (416). Or so he will tell Sosia (and us), after the narrative insert (412–15), as he points to that Sosia "here" romancing away on that story of what went down "there" (417–18), before turning directly to address "this" Sosia again (418).

416–22

416   **autumare** "affirm," a common verb in colloquial Latin texts

417   **illic** "there," adv.

    memorat memoriter "recounts in such a way that it shows a good memory" (which is why, so the "etymologically charged" jingle assures us, the word for recounting is so memorably welded to memory)

419   **qui** "from which," abl.

420   **e-locutus est** "he came *out* with the (*whole*) story." This time Sosia turns away to speak of his interlocutor for just an instant, in-between his interrogatives: so this "othering" in language, between actor and audience at the expense of an other actor, isn't working; instead it's getting sucked into the pseudo-exchange between actors that "really" addresses all the dramatic script to the audience.

421   **obsignata signo** "sealed up with a seal", so it truly *is* sealed;
       and the "seal" *is* the special "sign" it carries, the "symbol" that
       symbolizes its guarantee as a seal, plus its significance as a
       signifier. Yes, the colloquial over-insistence (here a thumping
       "figura etymologica") punches its weight, as usual.

       signi quid est "what, tell, (of a) seal-symbol is there?" (gen.
       "of respect")

       dic the imperative "tell," is here used appositionally (con-
       trast 391).

422   **me captas?** "are you trying to catch me (out)?"

Both Sosias have memorized the story (from the script, before
either appeared on stage; meanwhile, Jupiter is telling Alcmena the
same epic, in bed, so she can parrot it, too, back to her husband,
before he can tell her, 524–25, 744–46). Mercury is given his prompt
(418 ~ 260), and promptly delivers, word for word (419 ~ 261).

Here, however, is precisely the moment in the story where Sosia's
bulletin from the front gave out: *we* know, from Mercury in his role
as Prologue, where this "golden bowl" is now. (A dish for offering
obeisance and thanks to the gods for victory; and itself a symbolic offering, for safe return home, the wife's share of the spoils. It is tempt-
ing to think *patera* stands, in this annunciatory play with myth, for
"paternity," shared between Amphitryo and Ju-piter, though ancient
etymologists know only the link with *pateo*, "lie wide open." Well,
I'm tempted, and now I'm attempting to tempt you.) We know the
bowl is *not* in the casket; and now we know the seal is unbroken, and
know how come. When Amphitryo does get to present it to Alcmena
in person, she has already been given it, and given it by "him" (760–
97 ~ 534–36; cf. 421 ~ 787). By then, the early hints in our scene (386,
402, 448) that *insanity* is the only possible explanation, will have
ripened into a hallucinogenic cocktail of sorcery and witchery—and
earth-convulsing theogony.

The sign of "the rising solar chariot" heralds nativity . . . , "this is
the dawning of the age of . . . ," "it's a new day, it's a new dawn, and
a new life . . . ," and all that; but it's hard to miss "Count Dracula"

overtones in Jupiter's eagerness to leave his borrowed and vamped Queen and "get out of town before sun-up" (533, 543, cf. 737, 743). In a moment, Mercury will pull out the big gun and warn Sosia to stay out of the castle, or there'll be no escape, "not even if he mounts Jupiter's chariot" (450–51). Through the truly convulsive wreckage of the text in surviving manuscripts of *Amph*, which has shattered the climactic epiphany of the Almighty Father, it is surely impossible to imagine Jupiter come to deliver his blessing to both consort and "*commaritus*," for both savior demigod and his earthly twin sharing their cradle, on any other stage contraption than one helluva solar-powered chariot (making like the version that crowned the roof-top of Jupiter's Capitoline temple)? That's certainly how my blinder of a production would go—go out in a blaze of glory, hosanna-in the-highest.

423–32

429   **inde . . . hirneam** "a jug from here, i.e., from it."

ingressust = *ingressus est* (pf. of deponent verb *in-gredior*, "set foot on," "begin"). Once more, the interjection that "others" the speaker as he plays third-person narrator lasts a nanosecond—for all that this time the impersonator "has just set foot on the road (i.e., started)," whereas before he already "came *out* with the (*whole*) story" (429 ∼ 420). The way to direct the scene is to make sure that the pattern is hammed up by getting the actor to take up the same stance between his partner and the audience as he goes through the variations on the same "routines." The overall "tragi-comic" duplication involved in shifting from vamped-up heroics to camped-up anti-heroics, between "Sturm und Drang" saga and "Skulked and Drank" feat *has to* get across in our playhouse. But it's *also* hilariously wicked to be reminded here of Homer's traumatic *Iliad*, with its proud Achilles stuck in *his* tent for so long, while his comrades were outside dying in droves . . .

430   **eam ego, ut matre fuerat natum, uini eduxi meri** "I drained [smuggling in the sense "I trained," as in "raised (a child)"], of wine, pure as it was once born from its mother" (with *fuerat*

colloquial plupf. for impf., and *uini* gen. "of emptying"). Here's some high-falutin' high-style figure of speech, personifying the booze as one of the family. It is brought on by method-overacting the wine-loving slave.

431 **illic** "there," adv.

432 **mira sunt** "it's a wonder," to start the pile of proliferating miracles wrought by—the playwright.

  illic "he," pron.

The machinery of nationwide news and security technology have provided one set of winning "proofs" that Sosia is the one who has (A) the latest information not yet available and (B) privileged information that is withheld. A second winsome set (433 ~ 423) will "catch out" the pretender, privileged information in the form of private behavior, unmonitored and under cover.

First Sosia tells Sosia he needs to find a name "other" than Sosia, then he again tries othering the other Sosia by third-person-ing him with gesturing prons., "him here" who watched "that there" (like some spectator watching out there inside the theater): "Sosia-I will catch *him here* out, good" (424). "The other" is, however, still here right now, so Sosia needs to wheel in a somewhere else, a somewhen else, to absent "him" (425–26, *alius* ~ 423, *aliud*).

So Sosia turns to address "Sosia" (here, now), expecting he will fall for the battlefield scam also announced in that rehearsal speech, and cued for us here. What was he up to "when the legions were fighting their hardest"? (427 ~ 199) He will pretend he was there too (200), when actually "he was running his hardest" (199). Now he fills in the real scenario: "alone in his tent, no one around—what did he do?" Here is the battle for heart and mind, the "victory" that counts, and winner takes all! (428)

Anyone in the audience would guess booze must have come into it, so this "Cunning Slave" must play blind to "Sosia's" ability to "pretend he was there" and fake up his own report of the memorable scalp when the hero took on the might of a flagon of vino, solo, in man-to-can fighting. Truly, a surefire bet, and 100% "proof"! The perfect simulation of a Sosia's way of *speaking*, when owning (up to) his way of *sneaking*, clinches the impersonation, as both Sosias play rhyming Tweedledee and Tweedledumb (430 ~ 431). Between them, they contrive to match the previous argument, where the epic bowl inside the grand sealed casket, and an insider's knowledge of it, could not be accessible from outside. The comic twin argument puts a slave inside a tent and wine inside a jar; the slave takes the wine out and puts it inside a jug; then he takes the wine out of the jug and puts it inside himself. For any "other" one else to be in on this, they'd have to have been inside the jug—"the place from which he watched it (i.e., that *dramatic* magic-show)" (424, *spectauit*)—where no one could know he was around. What *we're* being let into here is the notion of getting "inside" someone else's head (as in the film *Being John Malkowitz*)—only the alien turns out to be our self. This *must* be an inside-job—no "if" or "if not" about it (427, *si* ~ 432, *nisi*).

433–40

<dl>
433   **uincon** = *uinco* + *ne*

434   **quid . . . ni negem, qui egomet siem?** "why would I, who am indeed (Sosia) deny (that I am Sosia) ?" The verb "to be" is here attracted into the subjunctive by association with the hypothetical question *quidni negem*?

438   **saltem** "at any rate," "in that case."

440   **ignobilis** "not known," "a stranger." This barb helps set us up for the "logical ultimate" of 461, *ignorabit*.
</dl>

"What now?" indeed (433). The tangled messing with prons. and persons is peaking—has won the arguments—by now. "You're not Sosia/Sosia's not you." "You say I'm not (Sosia/you) and (Sosia) isn't me/(you) aren't me." "Sure I say that (any and all those things that you say are so) are not (so), I who am indeed I (but am also saying that I am the 'me' you said you are as well as saying that I am the Sosia and Sosia is the me that you say 'I' am)." . . . As we (try) to turn away from the non-sense of imploded language as communication between humans, along with collapsed "proofs" and escaped "reason," we fall into invoking the gods as sanction on credibility. This means swearing in their name, and that means believing in/trusting (*credere*) the interlopers in the play; in the case of Sosia, formal appeal to higher witness and authority is another doomed attempt to finesse addressing the other party present (435). "I swear that I am (me? Sosia? etc., etc.), and I swear that I do not speak falsehood/I swear that it is not the false I (Sosia . . .) speaking/it is not the false I (etc.) that says (that I am I, etc.)." "Ye gods!" indeed, you might say.

But Mercury calls a halt, as deity tells humankind that God doesn't trust/believe them (436–37). The gods "know" not to trust earthling oaths, which are sworn to outbid other rhetorical power-plays (such as "argument"). The Almighty has no need of belief or trust, in any case, because he has the power: oaths don't cut it with him, from god or man. Maybe the gods are like us, anyhow, in simply siding with each other, with their like, and that is all that rhetorical moves are designed for, and designed to camouflage. But Jupiter will *not* go believing his son in any case, since he is the trickster god of lies as well as of communication, interpretation, language, of communication— and self-interest! For example, it's hard not to believe Mercury, even, for instance, when he tells us he is a comic slave, the comic slave Sosia, when we know he is only acting the part of the comic slave (Sosia) that (Sosia) the comic slave is acting.

Sosia asks "what I am I if not Sosia?" You could play his question as throwing in the towel, throwing himself on the mercy of the one who "knows" the answers; or as an objection, a fresh argument; or as another hint of a possible silver lining to Sosia's cloud. "If not Sosia, then who?—well, some "who," not no one, and someone, some who that doesn't have to be Sosia . . ." At any rate, Mercury eases a little—the identity theft needn't be on a permanent footing. *So the play may be able to quit this giant warm-up scene and get on to the "real" action*. And at the same time this so-and-so reverts to his bullying strategy, promising to beat Sosia out of all recognition (*uapulabis*, 440 = 379; cf. -*a*, 370, 395; -*em*, 388). But this time, the "if" and "if not" are moving the stakes along (438, *si*; 440, *ni*)—and Mercury will send Sosia packing, stage left. *So the scene will close with Mercury left on stage to soliloquize, in a "second Prologue," to re-start the play.* And imprint the pattern of doubling and redoubling, repeating and replicating, representing and reproducing. Amphitryo, *both* king, conqueror, and warrior, *and* head of household, husband, father-to-be, and owner-master, in one, is going to have his day, and have his play; at once an Agamemnon and a Pentheus (see **Further Reading**), and one more comic *senex*. And we are going to have him track, in high-and-mightily-fallen style, every move, wince, yelp, and grovel so lavishly choreographed and performed by his forerunner fallguy Sosia. The comedy will be a fantastic leveler, between gods and men as between humans. But not on a permanent basis, by Hercules! (And by his half-brother/twin!)

441–49

442   **quem ad modum** "in what way," "how"

nimis simile est mei "it is too, too like me" (with gen.). No point in deciding whether the "inspection" is funnier if the two Sosiae of our production look very different or cannot be told apart: in theater we both see what we're told to see and we carry on seeing whatever we see anyhow, just the same. The prologue very carefully instructed us that Sosia carries a lantern and Mercury has feathers in his hat so you can't miss which is which (and so too with the two Amphitryos: 142–45, 149–50). Funnier with a giant lantern and enormous feathers? And a way for Plautus to make the point I just put forward? There *is* nothing "objective"—outside language, desire, agenda, script—about the pet idea that anyone "looks like" anyone else (even their pet); no more than the idea that people "look different."

443   **tam consimilist** (= *consimilis est*) **atque ego** "he is as alike as I (am)!"

445   **quid uerbis opust?** lit. "what need is there of words?" i.e., "in short"

446   **nihil hoc simili est similius** "nothing is more like than this likeness"

448   **sane** "soundly"

   sapio "I have my senses, my wits about me." Sounds supple-
   ment senses, as Sosia wakes up his ideas, and reminds himself
   of what he knows he knows. So he must obey his own impera-
   tives, and get past that front door.

449   **non ego illi ob-tempero quod** "I'm not knuckling [= "going to
   knuckle"] down to anything that"

Sosia takes the initiative. This time he uses his loaf and the evidence of his eyes (441–42), again meaning to finesse dialogue and
the double-dealing of language (445, *quid uerbis opust*?). Naturally,
his prons. play him false some more ("when I contemplate *him* and
recognize *my* shape/appearance . . . , " 441), but he does make the
audience spectate along with him, in the most detailed description of
what we are to see standing before our very eyes on stage: the "complete" actor (445, *totus*; see *Marshall 133–34 for other such run-
downs). Only, of course, he *performs* this as a "me-and-my-shadow"
routine worthy of a Groucho Marx, measuring up each feature as
he plays up and down the body from hat to toe and then scrutinizes
head and face in close-up. Let's take the image of the "mirror-image"
as a stage-direction, to be mirrored in the acting, as one Sosia lookalike measures himself up against his "reflection." Naturally, we appreciate that these dead ringers are proving that gods look "just like"
something, and so do slaves (look like slaves-and-gods-looking-like-
slaves)—and *vice versa* (see especially 284). They are both an *act*.
And a *simulation*. Copies, let us say, without an original.

   Naturally the identikit only needs *itemizing*, since *description* is
superfluous for comparing like with like exteriors paraded bang in
front of us. Comedy is proud to present its grotesque wardrobe—
(yokel) hat and (funny) clothes, (fatty) shins and (clown) feet, (bent)
spine and (daft—shocking scarlet) wig, (slitty) eyes, (snub) nose,
(rubber) lips, (lantern) jaw, (pointy) chin, (scraggy) beard, (bull)
neck. This "recognition scene" with a difference—namely, that it is a
self-recognition scene, in which naming names is not going to clinch

a thing—momentarily apes its betters, in pointing out that superficial marks of identification—costume and looks, "externals" (= 441, *formam . . . meam*)—are poor guides to permanent selfhood.

Poor in comparison with the inside story, of what outsiders can't see—the concealed intimate body, represented in Homer's *Odyssey* by the hero's scarred thigh, indelibly imprinted on his nurse's memory. Naturally, "a scarred hide," even if we were given a good sighting of "weals on the back," could do *nothing* to individuate one comic slave from another, let alone one Sosia from the other (446). But the point of handing Sosia the opportunity for extended dialogue with himself (taking his time over the inspection, including asking and answering his own question, and repeating similar phrases as similarities check out) turns out to be to hand him the chance to perform the most intimate check-up you, or anyone else, can think of.

The mind-parasites may have stolen his personal knowledge and hacked into his private experience, but Sosia thinks aloud that he has indeed been thinking aloud, *while* contemplating and ticking the boxes (441). Which is to to say that when he says the words "when (or while) I am thinking," he is indeed thinking, and aware that he is thinking, and that "inspection" tells him it is him doing the thinking, so the thinking must be his, and he must be the thinker (and speaker). Even though his exclusive right to narrate the memory-track of his experience has been hijacked by the aliens, it feels like himself when he samples his thoughts and feels himself thinking that it sure feels permanent, and indeed when he says so (447). And this does come ludicrously close to the philosopher Descartes' in/famous in*tro*spection of the self as existing, beyond sceptical doubt, in and through the moment of thought: *cogito, ergo sum*. At the very least, you can't doubt that Plautus has thought—sceptically—about the dynamics of recognition.

Sosia gets a grip. Feel his elation. Back in the knowledge—the owner he's come from, belongs to, and the house he's come to, belongs in. The juices flow, the senses pulse. Forget the thing in the way. Take no orders from him, obey master's. See the house—see the door. Home! Go for it. Across the abyss. Knock, knock! (448–49, 450)

450–54

450   **quo | agis te?** "where you off to?"

451   **poteris** the mixed conditional clause treats "boarding Ju-
        piter's chariot" as unreal, but the possibility of "escape" as
        certainly null.

        in-fortunium this talk of "out-of-lucky-ness" dresses those
        iron fists in velvet glosses: Mercury reverts to re-doubled
        threats of physical violence (cf. 440).

453   **lumbi-fragium** "back-breaking," "back-wreck": a coinage?
        (Found only here and at *Cas* 968).

        nuntiare understand *licet* from 452

454   **irritassis** the "*s*-form" for pres. or pf. subjunctive

"Ifs" and "if *not*" (446, *si*, 450, *si*; 454, *si*, cf. 457, *si*, 461, *nisi*).
Mercury makes no clever-clever comeback, drops the persecution
personation jive, gets back to heavy-duty sentry-duty (cf. 150). Immediately before our passage started, he greeted Sosia with threats
of an unfriendly welcome and assisted exit "if he didn't go away,
pronto" (355, 357–58. 360). This he just reprised at 440; and it is
about to be clinched at 455.

This one last time he summons up Fancy Big Talk to get the same
message across once for all. He speaks now in Sosia's own terms, of
"running away" to "escape" any fight when the chips are down (451
~ 199, *fugiebam*), but at the same time he puts the frighteners on
with a sudden injection of Superpower Rhetoric. In his talk of beating it in "Jupiter's chariot," we recognize the other side of the play,
the other side of that door, inside the bedroom, inside the Queen's
body, between vagina/uterus: where we are going next, once we
shoo Sosia, to join in with the Almighty playing away. Jupiter will
be playing comic *senex amator*—but getting *his* end away because
he's Almighty, and getting away with it because this is a tragicomedy. Jupiter himself will shortly be leaving the helipad, smartish. To
make his getaway, before sunrise. But he'll be back—to "Bless the
Child who's got it All."

Our twosome repeat squabble a little, with "*my*"—"no, *yours*, but not *ours*" bickering, over whose mistress is entitled to which master's message, replacing "*our* home"—"*your* home?" (453–54 ~ 409–10), but this is eclipsed by Mercury's latest threat-and-promise, which rustles up a comic flourish of torturous verbal lumber to see off its twin, th' ethereal cosmic rocket launch. "Board the Chariot of God, and don't spare the horses: full speed to safety!" Or else: "cart off (do away with) your own brokeback body, when it's too late!" (454 ~ 450–51). Or else.

455–59

455   **abeo potius** "rather (than that), I'm off"

456   **im-mutatus** "changed into (something else)"

457   **illic** "there" (at the harbor), adv. Images of the dead ancestors were worn by hired understudies in élite Roman funeral processions. *Not* for the likes of slaves.

458   **fuerat** "which once was (mine)," another colloquial plupf. for impf.

459   "(A thing) is being done to me alive that no one will ever do for me when I'm dead."

So Sosia steps back, that is: forward, but disengaging ready to return whence he came, tail between legs. He turns one last time, away from his god self, reduced again to third-person cipher, towards the audience. In addressing the gods, he is once more playing into enemy hands, but there again, *really* he is communing with no one else but Sosia, him selves (455, *obsecro uostram fidem* ~ 373, *tuam fidem obsecro*; cf. 388). He rattles off another set of questions, but this time they end with the decision to quit, not to press on in (456–57, 460 ~ 403–7, 409). The thought that he must've "left himself" somewhere, and "now has forgotten where he forgot, and left, himself," re-traces the theme of his repeat attempts to own his memories, all the way back to his rehearsal—and memorization—of the message of victory that he was meant to come home and deliver to mistress. This tells him where he should go see if he can find those memories and pick up the threads of his lost identity once again (460).

He is escaping with body and soul intact, but feels he has "got lost—and died" (*perii*). In a daze, he feels he's attended his own funeral—he must be "dead alive—living dead" (*uiuo . . . mortuo*). The "inspection" was wrong-headed, because then he thought that both of them shared the identical shape/appearance, but now he decides he's lost it (456, *formam* ~ 441). And then he'd thought the "total" package totted up as an exact copy, but now the other owns his "whole" semblance (457, *omnem* ~ 445, *totus*). Tucked away here, there's a chance for him to understand what's happened, but he's in no fit state—yet awhile—to hear or think out the implication of his own word for it, "metamorphosis" (456, *immutatus*: he will resurrect the theory later, 846; cf. 121–23).

Instead the slave jokes at his own expense, at the sort of funeral he'll never receive, where aristocrats arranged for a procession of actors to kit up—get their costumes on—and impersonate both the deceased and his distinguished ancestors. Here the crucial part of the take-off was the "face mask," or *imago*, also the word for the face mask worn by characters on stage, tragic or comic (458, cf. 141). Once more high culture and low culture are brought together in our punsome tragicomedy—and we are reminded that all those facial details in the "inspection" scene were *bound* to match perfectly, so long as both "Cunning Slaves" wore the "same" mask that belonged to their stock role. By the same token, our Sosia can have lost neither physiognomy nor visage—let alone had his facial features rearranged (not even by those fists, 316–18), not so long as he's out on stage wearing costume and mask, at any rate. "Immortal gods!" Expect no "good faith" where the god of theft is concerned.

460–62

461   **faxit** the "*s*-form" of the pres. or pf. subjunctive

462   **ut . . . caluos capiam pilleum** "that I should put on the felt cap of freedom once I'm bald." Upon manumission, a slave shaved his head, and wore the *pilleus* until the hair grew back—free.

Now he's good and come to a dead end, Sosia will go back to base. Instead of delivering his messenger speech to mistress, he'll reverse charges and report to master. Instead of the practiced epic/communiqué of triumph he brought us and was bringing her, he'll turnaround with—the comic script we've just been watching/reading, of dumbfounded defeat, failure to carry out orders, the "Night of the Zombie" (to be re-told, in fact, at 599–628).

One last cheery thought, in this looking-glass world, it should all replay just the same when he gets back to the other end: he wasn't recognized on homecoming, so he should by rights be unrecognizable by master too (461). Which would mean—one last prayer to the Almighty—that our Sosia need play Sosia no more. Choosing who to be—à la Mercury (439)—would have its special compensation if you're a slave, with your grotesque peasant sombrero, scary wig and false facial hair. Choosing to be free, with all the "comic" slaphead and skullcap paraphernalia, for a (new) start.

Not that this slave, or more or less any sane one, could *really* think of melting away happily into a welcoming world. No, Sosia will stick with his King, and live up to his name, "Savior," so "Still Alive." Just as Mercury will serve God his Father.

Recommended Edition

Christenson, D. (2000) *Plautus, Amphitruo*, Cambridge University Press: Cambridge; Mahoney, D. (2004) *Plautus, Amphitryo*, Focus Classical Commentary: Newburyport, MA

Translation

Roche, P. (1968) *Three Plays by Plautus*, Bolchazy-Carducci: Wauconda, IL; Watling, E. F. (1975) *Plautus*, The Rope *and Other Plays*, Penguin: Harmondsworth.

Further Reading

*Moore ch. 6; Dupont, F. (1976) "Signification théatrale du double dans l'*Amphitryon* de Plaute," *Révue des Etudes Latines* 54: 129–41 (repr., in trans., as "The theatrical significance of duplication in

Plautus' *Amphitryo*," in *Segal). For real Roman issues acted out in the comedy, see Forehand, W. F. (1971) "Irony in Plautus' *Amphitryo*," *American Journal of Philology* 92: 633–51; Galinsky, G. K. (1966) "Scipionic themes in Plautus' *Amphitryo*," *Transactions of the American Philological Association* 97: 203–35. For linkage with contemporary Roman triumphalism, see Lelièvre, F. J. (1958) "Sosia and Roman epic," *Phoenix* 12: 117–24, O'Neill, P. (2003) "Triumph songs, reversal and Plautus' *Amphitryo*," *Ramus* 32:1–38. To appreciate how grand tragic theater handles "the same themes," everyone should go see or read Aeschylus' *Agamemnon*, where they are set to spark the most stupendous interrogation of the "original" emergence of justice into civic society; same goes for Euripides' mind-blowing explosion of tragic/comic ambivalence in his *Bacchae*: Stewart, Z. (1958) "The *Amphitryo* of Plautus and Euripides' *Bacchae*," *Transactions of the American Philological Association* 89: 348–73.

∾ 5 Curtains (twice)

Time to go; time to take stock. Another double take (cf. **1**). The scripts usually signal The End in a brisk finale from the cast, whether taking a bow as ensemble (**5A**), or letting the last actor speak for the whole production team (**5B**). Either way, the point is of course to give us a chance to show our appreciation; but the audience often gets it in the neck, by being told why they should clap, what we'll be clapping if we do, and what it will say about us if we don't (see *Sharrock ch. 5). So, put your hands together, for the *Plautus Reader*!

∾ 5A Captiui 1029–36
Clap Now

Meter: *trochaic septenarii* (**pp. 146–47**)

1029–36

1029   **ad pudicos mores** "to suit decency, and character"

1030 **subigitationes** "ride-ificating," i.e., "covering (as bull does cow)," especially "deflowering (virgin)." This "abstract" form is only found here, and looks to be coined to inaugurate the zany-sounding jingle of verbal nouns to come. The primary verb *sub-igo* brought "agricultural" tone to talk about sex.

amatio found only in Plautus, five times, mainly for "funetic" purposes (i.e., fun-from-phonetics): "luvifyin'."

1031 **pueri suppositio** the noun is used four times by Plautus, and just once elsewhere in this sense. It's stock-in-trade for comedy: "palm-off-ing a child" (**4A**). *Capt* does put its own spin on this—"a boy foisted on a father," but grown-up, and not to defraudify him (of money).

argenti circumductio "defraudating [by "leading round (the block)] of money." The word has some solid technical senses, but this one is pure comic slang, found only here, and presumably coined for this "Rhyme Time."

1032 **ubi amans adulescens scortum liberet** "where a lover-boy may set free [subjunctive] a whore." In fact, *Capt* does find room for some mini-adventures in the skin trade—but with a toy-*boy*, and on the side, by innuendo, *not* as mainspring of the plot.

clam svom patrem prep. + acc., "unbeknownst to his father." The father *does* get tricked by his son—but neither of them know it at the time.

1033 **huius modi . . . comoedias** "comedies of this sort". (*huius* scans as a monosyllable)

1034 **ubi boni meliores fiant** "where the good may become better"

1034-35 **si uobis placet | et si placuimus** this comedy is so polite, it hurts. These sweet-talking players merge the audience's "enjoyment" into their "en-judgement," as if on this mold-breaking occasion we are on some sober jury, not off the leash having fun.

1035 **odio fuimus** "we have been for (an object of) hate" ("predicative" dat.)

1036   **qui pudicitiae esse uoltis praemium** "(all) you who want
        there to be a pay-off for decency"

Anything up to the last quarter of a play may be devoted to Winding
Up Proceedings, long before we get anywhere near sight of the Wrap
Up. "Positive" plays like *Capt* (and *Rud*), and fiendishly complicated
feasts of "Cunning" (like *Pseud*), where we're to enjoy, and get lost in,
the settlement, take their time to find and tie all the loose ends going;
or else they career wildly through anything that might count as loose
(depending on how you direct the production—it's all in the timing).
At the other extreme, scripts can clear the stage with an abrupt "So Put
Your Hands Together" formula (especially *Curc*). Sometimes one actor
serves notice, turning mid-line to address the audience out of character; or as here the whole crew "Sing Out" together, as an "ensemble"
(*caterua*). There aren't rules for any of this, but plays that end up with
"Bags Packed Ready to Go" (*Men, Poen*) cease with the plaudit ("Call
for Applause"), whereas those where the characters go "inside" for the
backstage party regularly crack some sort of joke about it (*Pseud, Rud*:
there'll be room in bed for us, too, in *Truc*). One punk "Curtain Call"
throws in a ruffian dig at us, as the cast tell us not to hang around
waiting for them to take a bow, they're busy getting the job done "inside," before getting out of their costumes: "It's traditional for *you* to
'Show Your Appreciation' in the usual way!" (*Cist*).

Up to a point, *Capt* does set up against its own kind, and earns
this holier-than-thou sermonification against the nihilistic shame-
lessness of Plautine Comedy (already trumpeted by the prologue,
at 55–58, "no obscene lines, oath-breaking pimp, wicked hooker,
show-off soldier"). It is a "rarity," with "improving" characters by the
shipload, and could easily be offensive to audiences wanting a rest
from edifying theater (as *tragedy* was standardly billed, with whatever im/plausibility: another hint dropped by Prologue, at 58–62).
There is no sex, no lover-boy to free his sex-slave beloved (as in *Rud*.);
no smuggled-in-baby-hire (as in *Truc*), no financial shenanigans (as
in *Pseud*). Though "father" *has* been tricked by "son," and "liberation" *did* get a result, this all-male company has made fun by aping

the language of farce (as here, in its provocatively loaded run-down of Plautine themes, to make a stand-out Plautine "*Exeunt Omnes*" twist). That favorite "Good-Time Charlie," the Parasite (**3B**), gets a run-out, but strictly so he can be given the run-around. Above all, the "Cunning Slave," engine-room of Comedy (**3A**), doubles up to grab the limelight center-stage.

But here young master and loyal slave swap places, and stick to it, and though they do bamboozle the *senex*, this is done out of loyalty to the master-now-enslaved to a new common master; to say nothing of the fact that the master who plays slave was no slave in the first place, but rather a kidnapped child sold into slavery abroad, and in fact is the second son of the new master, to be this day reunited with his ransomed brother, who had himself been enslaved in war. Hence the non-mention of "Slave Plotting" in the epilogue's self-exorcism of farce is *both* deserved *and* a delusion! Relative naturalism marches hand-in-hand with subversive humanism in this liberating play where slavery is (precariously) denaturalized as the product of circumstances. As it was for hundreds of thousands of prisoners-of-war, the Greek-speaking "captives" of the Roman empire. To be sure, a play with "good" slaves is *also* a play with no "real" slaves, so *Capt* is more "offensive" to those who want their comedy "straight" than it is to any dreamer who thinks that slaves might be people "free" to be "good" (see *McCarthy in **Further Reading**). End of story.

Recommended Edition

Lindsay, W. M. (1900) *The* Captivi *of Plautus*, Macmillan: London; or use Nixon, P. (1916) *Plautus*, 1, Loeb Classical Library, Cambridge, MA: Harvard University Press.

Translation

Roche, P. (1968) *Three Plays by Plautus*, Wauconda, IL: Bolchazy-Carducci; Segal, E. in Slavitt, D. R., and Palmer Bovie eds. (1995) *Plautus, The Comedies*, 1, Baltimore: Johns Hopkins University Press; Watling, E. F. (1973) *Plautus*, The Pot of Gold *and Other Plays*, Harmondsworth: Penguin.

Further Reading

*Dunstan 165–73; *Konstan ch. 4; *McCarthy ch. 5; *Moore ch. 10; Leach, E. W. (1969) "Ergasilus and the ironies of the *Captivi*," *Classica et Medievalia* 30: 263–96; Thalmann, W. G. (1996) "Versions of slavery in the *Captivi* of Plautus," *Ramus* 25: 112–45.

5B Casina 1012–18
Or Else

Meter: *trochaic septenarii* (**pp. 146–47**)

1012–18

1013   **ex proxumo** "from next door"

1014   **nubet . . . nostro erili filio** "will marry . . . our master's [*erilis*, adj.] son"

1015   **manibus meritis** dat. and abl., "to" and "with hands that have earned it" (*manibus* in 1017 is abl.)

1016   **faxit** the "*s*-form" for pres. or pf. subjunctive

1018   **ei pro scorto supponetur hircus unctus nautea** "for him a billy-goat [= b. o.] anointed/smeared with bilge-water/gunk will be substituted in place of the whore"

This is the "naughty" variety of the "Clap Now" ending (also used for *Asin*), where we spectators are trapped into clapping our way into what *Capt* would pillory as "shameless ways." *Asin* instead invites you to get real and resist sanctimonious clap-trap, and own up to "Sympathy for the Devil." The cast there bids us to come off it and root for our anti-hero—you know you want to (943): "What he did was nothing new, weird, or off the way other characters behave." To get *their* dirty old man off from the beating his wife's about to hand him once she's hounded him back home (and to save the slave acting the Old Man's part a beating), clap now; and so play your own part, in demonstrating Comedy's vicarious investment in salacious slavering.

Bad Old *Cas* goes one better, as it bins the whole fuss and bother of dénouement with the throwaway line (1012): "I'll tell you what's going to happen inside." We never do get to see the "real" Babe, "Casina," so the Recognition Scene is junked, along with the business of her engagement to be married (1013–14). The prologue already warned us not to expect the groom-to-be to put in an appearance and save the day—"Plautus said no, broke down the bridge on his route," so no-show (64–66). We all know we've been had, because we must've wanted to get our paws all over Casina, same as the old goat *in Cas* . . . "O spectators," theater is, as you obviously agree, all about *punters, about johns, out ogling.* Wishing *we* had been in the movie—the way we are in our (erotic-fantasy) lives. Prologue *also* advertised Casina's immediate availability at reasonable rates, post-performance, backstage (84–86). But make no mistake, there's no such part, and if there were, she would have been played by another he in tights.

There *is*, however, one way we can get to grips with the play and use our hands . . . (1017). This time, people who put their hands together will get away with having their bought-in sex any time they like; and so the forfeit for clapping Plautus today is to accept typecasting as his "Old Lech." But those (males) who don't, and won't, out themselves this way are guaranteed top-billing in their very own reality show: there you'll be, up on top, with the hired honey just where you wanted her (the proverbial soft landing), and hey presto, there you'll be—going out with a bang—"humping a billy-goat awash with gunk" (1018). On which note—

Bibliography: See on **4B** (**pp. 90–91**).

Appendix A

❧ Divergences from the OXFORD CLASSICAL TEXT (of W. M. Lindsay [1904])

Plautus Reader: OCT

1A *Poen* 16: est : !esse!

2A *Curc* 477: maleuoli : maliuoli

2B *Poen* 560 se | : isq'se 561 aduenies (Bothe) : aduentes

3A *Pseud* 405 nusquam non : nunc nusquam 409 comprimunda est ... oratio : comprimunda ... oratiost

3B *Men* 85 compediti | anum : compediti ei anum 96 hunc : hunc nunc (Mueller) 100 ipsus; ... maxumae : ipsus ... maxumae, 105 caris : careis

3D *Men* 355 amantium : amantum 360 alloquar ultro : atque ultro alloquar 364 *lacuna* : omitted 365–66 tibi est ... mora : tibi ... morast (Leo)

4A *Truc* 485 pote : potest 487 retained : bracketed 488 deleted : non placet quem illi plus laudant qui audiunt quam qui uident (Guyet) 495 uirtute : uirtuti 503 euge : eugae 509 erre : !ere! 519 quique mihi : !quiquem ibi! 525 sauium pete hinc sis (Bothe) : sauium sis !pete! 526 egomet doleo (Spengel) : ego !medulo! 528 pigeat (Bothe) : pigeat [me] 531 his : is 535 cedo tu mi istam purpuram (Bothe and Bücheler) : cedo tu istam, puere, perulam 539 addi purpuram : purpuram 541 accipe hoc, Astaphium, abduce (Bach) : accepi hoc; abducite (Bothe)

4B *Cas* 799 meo : mi 802 nili : nihili 806 suffundam (Leo) : !si! offendam 807 adiuuabo : adiutabo 814B PA : CH 827 tu : tun (Lindsay) 828 | id quaerunt uolunt : id | quaerunt, id uolunt 829–30 uis uxorem, accipe : uis, uxorem accipe 834 ite iam. CL ualete : ite. CL. iam ualete. 847 pectus est (Geppert) : !est pectus!

4C *Asin* 758 amicae suae (Gulielmius) : amicai eum 785 post si : postid (Lindsay)

4D *Rud* 942 rete : retem 947 manedum (Leo) : modo 948 eloquere : eloqueren 961 etiam amplius (Seyffert) : etiam plus 984 rete : retem 1037 euge : eugae

4E *Amph* 393 mihi : mi 400 nobis praeter med : praesente nobis 401 deleted (Leo) : qui cum | Amphitryone hinc fueram in exercitum 408 nunc mihi : mi misero 443 consimilist : consimilest

Appendix B

∾ Meter

I find the commentaries of Gratwick on *Men* (**p. 67**) 40–63, 251–60 and MacCary and Willcock on *Cas* (**p. 90**) 211–32 the best help for understanding, scanning, and reading Plautine verse: both are model presentations, attempting to teach from first principles to expertise in a few short pages. A short profile here will give a fair idea of how these plays swing and thump along. (See **p. xii**.)

The mass of each script is "sing-song/talk," written in Plautus' favorite (most common) regular meters (= **1.1** and **1.2** below). The lines feel extremely "free" (like some talking blues). They play off the drive of spoken intonation against the recurrence of chanted half-line and whole-line units; each line is "called home" by a regular verse-end cadence. In iambic septenarii the words' own ordinary accentuation reinforces the verse cadence; in the other meters, there is often a clash between the two patterns. Across the length of the line, the sub-unit, or *metron*, of each verse has no underlying metronomic pulse. Thus a senarius can last anywhere between a light run of *alternating* short and long syllables (= 18 time-units, where a long lasts twice as long as a short) and a heavy run of *continuous* long syllables (= 23 time-units). Most senarii are of 22 units, with one short syllable at either the first or the second *c* (a notation to be explained next): but enough lines have 21 or 23 units to downplay this norm, and, while 19 (and especially 18) unit lines are far between, the few 20-unit verses are a significant minority. The final metron of *every* verse ends with a short syllable before a final long (so no senarius can ever last for 24 time units). The longer lines work correspondingly further away from internal or overall "isochrony" (= equal number of time units between metra or per line).

∾ *1. Iambic-trochaic verse*

N.B. In each metron, "B" and "D" are always long, "a" and "c" are those tending to be long or short ("a" mostly long; "c" rather more longs than shorts). Any element may be *either* a long syllable *or* two short syllables except at line-end: here the final two syllables are always short followed by long, except in iambic septenarii, where the final two syllables are always long followed by long. Within these parameters, the verse abides by a complex of norms for relating syllable patterns to spoken accentuation; these norms all have their exceptions, and never explain *all* the lines, or all the words. Editing Plautus is forever a test of nerve in tolerating or eliminating transmitted anomalies and violations, in meter as in all other aspects. As with any formal poetry, *reading* Plautus is always an ongoing negotiation between the pull of verse and the impetus of word accentuation.

1.1. Short spoken verse.
Iambic senarius, 1A, 1B; 3A, 3B; (4B: 780–97, 847–54), 4C:

   aBcDa BcDaBcD   *or*   aBcDaBc DaBcD

Usually with a word-break between *linked* "half-lines." The final "c" is *always* a "short" syllable. This is a conversational and so colloquial idiom but, as the *Reader* shows, it is capable of carrying a wide range of tones—most notably the legalistic formulae for the contractual clauses of **4C**.

1.2. Longer recitative verse.
Trochaic septenarius, 2A (462–85), 2B; 4A, (4B: 798–99, 801–7, 809–14), (4D: 963–1044), 4E; 5A, 5B:

   BcDaBcDa BcDaBcD

As if a "cretic" (or "long-short-long" pattern) is followed by an iambic senarius.

Here, any element may be resolved into two short syllables *except at mid-verse and verse-end*: cadences with "cD" have the penultimate syllable short; cadences in "BC" and "Da" have the penultimate syllable long; the final syllable of every verse counts as long.

This is Plautus' rhythm of choice, verses long enough to feel close to a double line—"two-for-the-price-of-one," you might say. This is why Plautin theater is all gabble and patter, all babble and clatter.

1.3. Other long recitative verse forms.

First, iambic octonarius, (2A: 486); (4D: 938–44):

aBcDaBcD aBcDaBcD   *or*   aBcDaBcDa BcDaBcD

These are the longest lines and, as in our passage, pay out enough rope to fight over.

Second, iambic septenarius, (4D: 945–46):

aBcDaBcD aBcDaBC

As if an octonarius minus its last syllable. These two lines are part of the shake-up in a metrical tug-of-war.

∾ *2. Sung and scored lyric verse*

Mixed meters, 3C, 3D; 4B, 4D:
For line-by-line metrical "conspectus" of all the plays, see the *Oxford Classical Text* of W. M. Lindsay (1904), vols. 1 and 2, at the end. On our four passages:

3C *Cistellaria* 203–29: Lindsay, as above

3D *Menaechmi* 351–69: see Gratwick (**p. 67**) 249

4B *Casina* 800, 808, 815–46: see MacCary and Willcock (**p. 90**) 185, 188–89

4D *Rudens* 947–62b: Lindsay, as above.

Illustration Credits

Fig. 1 King's Visualisation Lab, King's College London. With permission. Thanks to Prof. Richard C. Beacham, FRSA, Director, King's Visualisation Lab. The stage is based upon a mural in room 23 of the Roman Villa at Oplontis (see Richard C. Beacham, *Spectacle Entertainments of Early Imperial Rome*, New Haven and London: Yale University Press, 1999: 28).

Fig. 2 Map of the second-century BCE Roman Forum. Mapping Specialists, Ltd. © copyright 2009, Bolchazy-Carducci Publishers, Inc.

Fig. 3 Scene of three actors from a comedy (Atellan farce). Fresco from "The House of Casca Longus," Pompeii (I.6.11), housed in the Museo Archeologico Nazionale, Naples, Italy. Photo: Erich Lessing/Art Resource, NY.

Fig. 4 Original found on Lemnos (? Third century BCE. Height: 23.5 cm): Antikensammlung, Staatliche Museen zu Berlin / TC 7820. Photo: Karin März (copyright: bpk / Antikensammlung, Staatliche Museen, Berlin. Photo: Karin März). With permission. Thanks to Norbert Ludwig, Direktor, bpk (Bildarchiv Preußischer Kulturbesitz: Bildagentur für Kunst, Kultur und Geschichte).

Fig. 5 Photo: Cambridge Arts Theatre. Brad Fitt and Julie Buckfield in *Dick Whittington*, directed by Brad Fitt, Cambridge Arts Theatre, 2009–10. With kind permission from the Cambridge Arts Theatre. Special thanks to Nikki Hupe.

Fig. 6 Photo: James H. May, from 2003 production of *Rudens* at St. Olaf College, Northfield, Minnesota. With kind permission.

Vocabulary

ā/ab/abs, *prep.* + *abl.*, from, by

ab-aliēnō (1), sell ("make someone else's [property]")

ab-dūcō, -ere, abdūxī, abductum, lead away, take away

ab-eō, abīre, abiī, abitum, go away

ab-iūdicō (1), award as someone else's

ab-ripiō (rapiō), -ere, abripuī, abreptum, snatch away

abs-cēdō, -ere, abscessī, abscessum, retire, go away

abs-tergeō, -ēre, abstersī, abstersum, wipe off/away

abs-trūdō, -ere, abstrūsī, abstrūsum, shove away, hide

ac = atque, especially before a consonant

ac-cēdō, -ere, accessī, accessum, approach (with *dat.* or *ad*)

ac-cipiō (capiō), -ere, accēpī, acceptum, receive

ac-cubō, -āre, -itum, lie beside, go to bed with

aciēs, -ēī, *f.*, sharp edge

āctūtum, *adv.*, immediately

ad, *prep.* + *acc.*, towards, to, near, for, à la

ad-dīcō, -ere, addīxī, addictum, assign to (highest bidder), deliver

ad-dō, -ere, addidī, additum, put onto, add

ad-dūcō, -ere, addūxī, adductum, lead up, bring over

ad-eō, *adv.*, to this far, besides

ad-eō, adīre, adiī, aditum, go to, approach

ad-hibeō (habeō), -ēre, adhibuī, adhibitum, bring to, apply

ad-hūc, *adv.*, up to here, still

ad-iciō (iaciō), -ere, adiēcī, adiectum, throw in, add on

ad-iuuō (1), help

ad-moueō, -ēre, admōuī, admōtum, move up close to

ad-nuō, -ere, adnuī, adnūtum, nod yes, agree

ad-sum, adesse, affuī, am here

ad-uehō, -ere, aduexī, aduectum, convey to, fetch

ad-ueniō, -īre, aduēnī, aduentum, come to, arrive at

ad-ulēscēns (olēscō), -ntis, *m.*, teenager ("growing up [lad]")

ad-uocō (1), call to help (especially with legal defence); **advocātus**, *m.*, legal support

ad-uorsum/-us, *adv.*, facing, opposite ("turned-to-face")

ad-uortō, -ere, aduortī, aduorsum, turn towards

aedēs/-is, *f.*, shrine, (*pl.*) house

aeger, -gra, -grum, *adj.*, weak, ill

aequos, -a, -om, *adj.*, equal, fair; **-issumus, -a, -um**, *superl. adj.*, fairest; **-ē**, *adv.*, equally (with **atque** = "on a par with")

aes, -ris, *n.*, bronze, coin, cash

aestuō (1), boil

af-fatim, *adv.*, enough (lit. "to saturation")

af-ferō, afferre, attulī, allātum, bring to, fetch

af-flīgō, -ere, afflīxī, afflīctum, smash (to the ground)

age-dum, *see* **agō**

ag-itō (1), keep driving, stir up

agō, -ere, ēgī, āctum, drive, carry off, do; **nīl agō**, "get nowhere"; **quid agō**, "how am I doing?"; **age-dum**, *imperative*, come on now

āh, *interjection*, ah!

āiō, "*defective*" *verb*, say yes, say

ali-ēnō (1), make other, sell to someone else

ali-ēnus, -a, -um, *adj.*, of another, someone else's

ali-quis, -is, -id, *indefinite adj. and pron.*, some, any; someone/thing-or-other

ali-unde, *adv.*, from another place

alius, -a, -ud, *adj. or noun*, other or another person/thing

al-loquor, -ī, allocūtus sum, speak to, address

alō, -ere, aluī, altum, sustain, rear

alter, -a, -um, *adj. or noun*, one of a pair

am-ātiō, -ōnis, f., "lovifying," sex

am-ātor, -ōris, *m.*, lover

amb-itiō, -ōnis, f., going round (lobbying)

ambo, -ae, -o, *adj.*, both

ambulō (1), walk

am-īca, -ae, f., mistress ("female friend")

ā-mittō, -ere, āmīsī, āmissum, send away, let go

amō (1), love/lust for; **amāns, -ntis**, *pres. pple.* used as *noun*, lover; **amābō**, *fut. indicative*, "I'll love ya (if you do what I want)," "please"

amoen-itās, -ātis, f., loveliness/sexiness

a-mōmum, -ī, n., cardamom (a spice from Asia; naturalized Greek *amōmon*, "faultless[ness itself]")

am-or, -ōris, *m.*, love/lust

amplius, *compar. adv.*, more fully

an, *conj.*, whether, or

an-ceps (ambi-caput), -ipitis, *adj.*, double/split, doubtful ("bothsides-headed")

ancilla, -ae, f., maid

animu-lus, -ī, *m.*, "mind-i-kins," "soulmate"

animus, -ī, *m.*, mind

annus, -ī, *m.*, year

ante, *adv.*, in front; *prep.* + *acc.*, in front of

ant(e)-hāc, *adv.*, before-this, before

ante-pōnō, -ere, anteposuī, antepositum, put before

antid-eō (ante eō), antidīre, "*defective*" *verb*, outdo ("go before")

ānu-lus, -ī, *m.*, (finger-)ring

ānus, -ī, *m.*, ring, band

aperiō, -īre, aperuī, apertum, open

ap-pellō, -ere, appulsī, appulsum, push/drive to

ap-petō, -ere, appetiī/-īuī, appetītum, seek for, attack

ap-properō (1), hurry up

apud, *prep.* + *acc.*, at (the house of)

arbiter, -trī, *m.*, witness, third-party (to decide dispute)

arbitr-ārius, -a, -um, *adj.*, optional, discretionary

arbitr-ātus, -ūs, *m.*, opinion, choice

argentum, -ī, *n.*, silver, cash

argū-mentum (arguō), -ī, *n.*, proof, evidence

argū-tus, -a, -um, *adj.*, clear-voiced, incisive; **-ē**, *adv.*, cleverly

ariēs, -etis, *m.*, ram

arti-fēx, -icis, *m.*, artiste ("art-maker")

artus, -a, -um, *adj.*, squeezed, tight

a-spiciō (ad-speciō), -ere, aspexī, aspectum, look at, catch sight of

as-sentiō, -īre, assēnsī, assēnsum, agree with

as-serō, -ere, asseruī, assertum, join to, claim (as one's property, especially a slave)

as-seruō (1), watch over, observe/guard

as-simulō (1), liken

a-stō (ad-stō) -āre, astitī, stand by

a-strīngō (ad-strīngō), -ere, astrīnxī, astrīctum, bind up, bind tight

at, *conj.*, but, yet

āter, -tra, -trum, *adj.*, black

at-que, *conj.*, and; as *correlative*, . . . as/than

at-tineō (teneō), -ēre, attinuī, attentum, hold to, pertain to

at-tollō, -ere, "*defective*" *verb*, lift up high

at-trepidō (1), hustle along

audāc-ia, -āī (*archaic gen.*), *f.*, daring, recklessness

aud-āx, -cis, *adj.*, daring; **-cter**, *adv.*, boldly

audeō, -ēre, ausus sum, dare, am prepared to, am willing to

audi-entia, -ae, *f.*, hearing, attention

audiō, -īre, audiī/-īuī, audītum, hear

au-ferō (ab-ferō), auferre, abstulī, ablātum, carry away/off

au-fugiō (ab-fugiō), -ere, aufūgī, run away

augeō, -ēre, auxī, auctum, increase, build up

aur-eus, -a, -um, *adj.*, golden

aurī-tus (auris), -a, -um, *adj.*, "eared"

aurum, -ī, *n.*, gold

aut, *conj.*, or/either

autem, *particle*, but

autumō (1), say (yes), affirm

barba, -ae, *f.*, beard

basil-ica, -ae, *f.*, portico used as mart (naturalized Greek, "king's [hall]")

belli-atulus, -a, -um, *adj.*, prettykins-please

bellu-lus, -a, -um, *adj.*, pretty-please

bel-lus, -a, -um (bonus), *adj.*, pretty ("good little"); -ē, *adv.*, prettily

bibō, -ere, bibī, bibitum, drink

bīs, *adv.*, twice

bonus, -a, -um, *adj.*, and *noun*, good, good people, good thing/blessing

cadus, -ī, *m.*, wine jar (naturalized Greek *kados*)

caecus, -a, -um, *adj.*, blind

caedō, -ere, caesī, caesum, chop, cut

caluos, -a, -om, *adj.*, bald

campus, -ī, *m.*, plain,

canālis, -is, *m.*, channel, drain

can-ōrus, -a, -um, *adj.*, singing, tuneful

can-tus, -ūs, *m.*, singing

capiō, -ere, cēpī, captum, take, capture

capit-āl (caput), -is, *n.*, serious crime, something that carries the ultimate penalty ("punishment by loss of caput" = social death)

capt-iō, -ōnis, *f.*, attempt to catch, trick

captī-uos, -a, -om, *adj.*, and *noun*, captured, captive

capt-ō (capiō) (1), try hard to capture, catch out

caput, -itis, *n.*, head

careō, -ēre, caruī, lack, be without (with *abl.*)

carnu-fex, -icis, *m.*, butcher, executioner (term of abuse; = "meat-doer")

carnu-ficīna, -ae, *f.*, torturer's trade

cārus, -a, -um, *adj.*, dear

catēna, -ae, *f.*, chain

caterua, -ae, *f.*, troop/troupe

catus, -a, -um, *adj.*, canny

caueō, -ēre, cāuī, cautus sum, beware (of = *abl.*)

causa, -ae, *f.*, cause, reason; -ā, *prep. + gen.*, for the sake of

-ce, *"enclitic" particle*, this here

ce-do, *imperative*, "gimme"

celōx, -ōcis, *f.*, "schooner"; as if *adj.*, swift

cēna, -ae, *f.*, dinner

cēnō (1), have dinner

cēnseō, -ēre, cēnsuī, cēnsum, reckon

cēra, -ae, f., wax

cēr-ātus, -a, -um, adj., waxed

cerebrum, -ī, n., brain

cerrītus, -a, -um, adj., crazy

certus, -a, -um, adj., certain, sure; -ē/-tō, adv., certainly, for sure

cibus, -ī, m., food

cicātrīc-ōsus, -a, -um, adj., (heavily) scarred

circum-duct-iō, -ōnis, f., defrauding (by "leading round [the block]")

cistu-la, -ae, f., little chest, casket

citior (cieō), -ior, -ius, compar. adj., faster, sooner

cīuis, -is, m., citizen,

clam, adv., secretly; prep. + acc., unbeknown to

clāmō (1), yell

clārē, adv., clearly

clāuos, -ī, m., nail

clueō, -ēre, "defective" verb, am known as ("hear myself called")

clupeus, -ī, m., shield

cōgitō (1), think

cognōscō (cum-gnōscō), -ere, cognōuī, cognitum, get to know, realize

colaphus, -ī, m., punch (naturalized Greek)

col-lātor, -ōris, m., fetcher, contributor

col-laudō (1), praise highly

collum/-us, -ī, n./m., neck

color, -ōris, m., color

columen, -inis, n., ridge-pole (supporting a roof), "keystone," "crowning glory"

com-būrō, -ere, cōmbussī, cōmbustum, burn up

com-edō, comēsse, comēdī, comēsum, eat up

com-itium, -iī, n., assembly place for Roman elections

com-marītus, -ī, m., "co-groom"

com-mentor, -ārī, commentātus sum, meditate, practice speaking/taking off

com-min-īscor, -ī, commentus sum, think up, invent

com-mōnstrō (1), point right at, show

com-moueō, -ēre, commōuī, commōtum, move about, jiggle

com-mūnis, -is, -e, adj., common, shared

cōm-oedia, -ae, f., comedy (naturalized Greek)

com-par, -ris, adj. and noun, equal, matching; mate, other half

com-parō (1), compare

com-pedēs, -um, f. pl., shackles (for feet)

com-pediō, -īre, compedīuī, compedītum, shackle

com-plicō (1), wind up

com-pōnō, -ere, composuī, compositum, put together, compose

com-pressus, -ūs, *f.,* squashing, having sex with (man-on-woman)

com-primō, -ere, compressī, compressum, squeeze together, restrain

con-cēdō, -ere, concessī, concessum, yield, withdraw

con-celebrō (1), throng, make it buzz

con-cinnō (1), fit together, get ready

con-demnō (damnum) (1), condemn

con-diciō, -ōnis, *f.,* condition

con-dō, -ere, condidī, conditum, put, stick

cōn-ferō, cōnferre, contulī, collātum, bring together, fetch

cōn-fīdō, -ere, cōnfīsus sum, trust in, believe (with *dat.*)

con-iectūra (iactō), -ae, *f.,* estimate

cōn-scrībō, -ere, cōnscrīpsī, cōnscrīptum, write up

cōn-sequor, -ī, cōnsecūtus sum, follow up, make for

cōn-sil-ium, -siliī, *n.,* advice, plan

cōn-similis, -is, -e, *adj.,* very like (with *dat.*)

cōn-spec-tus, -ūs, *m.,* viewing

cōn-stō, -āre, cōnstitī, stand firm, cost

cōnsul-ō, -ere, cōnsuluī, cōnsultum, take counsel

cōn-suō, -ere, cōnsuī, cōnsūtum, sew together, cobble together (a plan)

con-templō (1), observe (usually *deponent*)

con-tinuos (teneō), -a, -om, *adj.,* continuous ("holding together"); **-ō,** *adv.,* without a gap, instantly

contrā, *adv.,* against

con-tumēlia, -ae, *f.,* abuse, insult

con-tundō, -ere, contudī, contūsum, beat to a pulp, hammer

con-ueniō, -īre, conuēnī, conuentum, come together, meet (with *dat.*)

con-uincō, -ere, conuīcī, conuictum, defeat, convict

con-uīua, -ae, *m.,* dinner-guest

con-uīuium, -iī, *n.,* dinner

con-uortō, -ere, conuortī, conuorsum, turn, change

cōpia, -ae (co[n]-ops), *f.,* abundance, wherewithal, funding, chance for/sexual access to (with *gen.*)

coquō, -ere, coxī, coctum, cook

coquos, -ī, *m.,* cook

corbīta, -ae, *f.,* barge

cor-culum, -ī, *n.,* heartikin

corium, -iī, *n.,* hide

corōna, -ae, *f.,* crown, garland (naturalized Greek)

corpus, -ōris, *n.,* body

corpus-culum, -ī, *n.,* "body-kins"

crās, *adv.,* tomorrow

crēdō, -ere, crēdidī, crēditum, believe, trust (with *dat.*)

crepō, -āre, crepuī, crepitum, rattle, creak

cruciā-bilitās (crux), -ātis, *f.*, agony

crucio (1), torture ("crucify")

cubi-culum, -ī, *n.*, bedroom

cubitum, -ī, *n.*, elbow

cubō, -āre, **cubuī**, **cubitum**, lie down; **cubitum eō**, go to bed (to have sex)

cum and **-cum**, *prep.* + *abl.*, with

cūnctō (1), delay, hesitate

cupiō, -ere, **cupiī**/-**īuī**, **cupitum**, desire

cūr, *interr. adv.*, why?

cūr-ātor, -ōris, *m.*, manager ("carer")

cūrō (1), care for, take care of

cur-sor (currō), -ōris, *m.*, runner

damn-ōsus, -a, -um, *adj.*, damaging, spendthrift ("harm-full")

dapsilis, -is, -e, *adj.*, richly-endowed (Greek *dapsilēs*)

dē, *prep.* + *abl.*, down from, about

dea, -ae, *f.*, goddess

decem, *numeral*, 10

decet, -ēre, **decuit**, *impers. verb*, it is becoming, befitting

dē-cipiō (capiō), -ere, **dēcēpī**, **dēceptum**, catch, deceive

decum-us, -a, -um, *adj.*, 10th

decus, -oris, *n.*, glory

dē-ferō, **dēferre**, **dētulī**, **dēlātum**, carry off, fetch

dē-ligō (1), bind up

dē-lūdō, -ere, **dēlūsī**, **dēlūsum**, make fun of

dē-mittō, -ere, **dēmīsī**, **dēmissum**, let down

dē-mō (dē-emō), -ere, **dēmpsī**, **dēmptum**, take away

dēnuō (dē nouō), *adv.*, afresh, again ("from new")

dē-scendō (scandō), -ere, **dēscendī**, **dēscēnsum**, climb down, get down from

dē-serō, -ere, **dēseruī**, **dēsertum**, unlink, leave behind

dē-spoliō (1), strip off

dē-tergeō, -ēre, **dētersī**, **dētersum**, wipe off

dēterior, -ōris, *compar. adj.*, worse

dē-texō, -ere, **dētexuī**, **dētextum**, finish off weaving

dē-tineō (teneō), -ēre, **dētinuī**, **dētentum**, held off, detain

dē-ueniō, -īre, **dēuēnī**, **dēuentum**, come down to

deus, -ī, *m.*, god (*pl.*, **dī**)

dīcō, -ere, **dīxī**, **dictum**, say

diēs, -ēī, *f.*, day

dif-ferō, **differre**, **distulī**, **dīlātum**, carry off in different directions, tear apart

digitu-lus, -ī, *m.*, finger-let

dī-midium (medius), -iī, *n.*, half

dī-ripiō (rapiō), -ere, **dīripuī**, **dīreptum**, rip apart

dī-rumpō, -ere, **dīrūpī**, **dīruptum**, smash apart

discō, -ere, **didicī**, learn

dis-sīgn-ātor, -ōris, *m.*, assigner, usher to seats

dis-suādeō, -ēre, dissuāsī, dissuāsum, advise against, talk out of

dis-trahō, -ere, distrāxī, distrāctum, pull apart

diū, *adv.*, by day (*abl.* of **diēs**); long/for a long time;

dīues/dīs, -īuitis/-ītis, *adj.*, wealthy

dī-uidō, -ere, dīuīsī, dīuīsum, divide

dō, dare, dedī, datum, give

doceō, -ēre, docuī, doctum, teach

doleō, -ēre, doluī, dolitum, am in pain

dolor, -ōris, *m.*, pain

dolus, -ī, *m.*, cunning, plot (naturalized Greek)

domi-nus, -ī, *m.*, master of household

domītus sum: nonce word, "home-d"

domō, -āre, domuī, domitum, tame

domus, -ūs/-ī, *f.*, house, household; **-um** (*acc.*) home(ward); **-ī** (*locative*), at home

dōnō (1), present with a gift

dōnum, -ī, *n.*, gift; **-ō,** *dat.*, for/ as a gift

dormiō, -īre, dormiī/-iuī, dormītum, sleep

dubitō (1), am in doubt, hesitate

dūcō, -ere, dūxī, ductum, lead, take away

dūdum, *adv.*, for a long time, long since

duellum, -ī, *n.*, war

dum, *conj.*, while, so long as; **-dum,** *"enclitic" particle*, a mo'

duo, -ae, -o, *numeral*, two

du-plex, -icis, *adj.*, double(- edged)

du-plicō (1), double

dūrus, -a, -um, *adj.*, hard/harsh

e/ex, *prep.* + *abl.*, from, out of

eapse = **ipsa**

ē-bibō, -ere, ēbibī, ēbibitum, drink up

ē-castor, *"expletive" interjection*, "Sure, by Castor!" (a common colloquial intensifier used by women)

ecc-um (ecce-hunc), -am, -ōs, -ās, *demonstrative adj.* or *pron.*, him/her/them there

ec-quī, -ae, -od, *interr. adj.* and *pron.*, *any* and *any*one/ *any*thing?

ec-quis, -is, id, *interr. adj.* and *pron.*, *any* and *any*one/ *any*thing?

ede-pol, *"expletive" interjection*, "Sure, by Pollux!" (a very common intensifier in conversational Latin)

ē-dīcō, -ere, ēdīxī, ēdictum, decree

edō, ēsse, ēdī, ēsum, eat

ēduc-ō (1), bring up, educate

ē-dūcō, -ere, ēdūxī, ēductum, draw from, drain; bring up, train

ef-fodiō, -ere, effōdī, effossum, dig up

ef-fugiō, -ere, effūgī, run away, escape

ego, meī, mihi/mī, mē/mēd, mē, *pron.*, I, me

ego-met, *pron.*, I (emphatic, insistent)

ehem , *interjection*, ah!

eho, *interjection*, hey!

ēī, *interjection*, oh no! with *dat.*, alas for; **ēī,** *dat. sing.* or *nom. pl.* of **is**

ē-loquor, -ī, ēlocūtus sum, speak out

ē-mentior, -īrī, ēmentītus sum, lie (big time)

ē-mittō, -ere, ēmīsī, emissum, send out

emō, -ere, ēmī, ēmptum, buy

ē-nicō (nex), (1), kill dead

enim, *conj.*, for ("look—there!")

enim-uērō, *conj.*, indeed, "for truly"

ēn-umquam, *adv.*, *never-ever?* ("look—ever?")

eō, īre, iī/iuī, itum, go

eō, *adv.*, there, on that account (*abl.* of **is**)

epistula, -ae, *f.*, letter (naturalized Greek *epistolē*)

e-quidem, *particle*, yes indeed (especially = "I am so")

equos, -ī, *m.*, horse

era, -ae, *f.*, owner, mistress

ergō, *adv.*, so, therefore

erīlis, -is, -e, *adj.*, belonging to owner (of slaves)

erre, *imperative*, "Off you go" (from Greek verb *errō*)

erus, -ī, *m.*, owner, master (of slaves)

ēs-ca (edō), -ae, *f.*, food, bait

ēsc-ārius, -a, -um, *adj.*, of eating

ēs-uriō (edō), -īre, ēsurītum, "*defective*" *verb*, want to eat, am hungry

et, *conj.*, and, even

et-iam, *particle*, still, even, also

et-sī, *conj.*, even if, although

euax, *interjection*, yippee! (naturalized Greek)

euge, *interjection*, yeah! (naturalized Greek)

ex-āmen (ag-men), -inis, *n.*, swarm, host

ex-animō (1), force the life out of

ex-cīdō (caedō), -ere, excīsī, excīsum, chop up

ex-cipiō (capiō), -ere, excēpī, exceptum, catch (from), receive

ex-cutiō (quatiō), -ere, excussī, excussum, shake out/off

ex-eō, exīre, exiī/-īuī, exitum, go/come out

ex-erceō (ex-arceō, "keep right away, keep at it"), **-ēre, exercuī, exercitum,** work at

ex-erci-tus (ex-arceō), -ūs, *m.*, army

ex-imo (emō), -ere, exēmī, exēmptum, take out, remove

ex-itium, -iī, *n.*, coming out

ex-ol-ēscō, -ere, exolēuī, exolētum, grow up, to full bloom/past best, clap out

ex-optō (1), wish for

ex-ōrdior, -īrī, exōrsus sum, set up loom for weaving, begin

ex-orior, -īrī, exortus sum, rise up (from)

ex-pediō, -īre, expedīuī, expedītum, set free (from shackles), free up

ex-perior, -īrī, expertus sum, try out,

ex-petō, -ere, expetiī/-īuī, expetītum, seek out

expōnō, -ere, exposuī/īuī, expositum, lay out, flatten

ex-pōrgō = exporrigō (i.e., ex-pro-regō), -ere, exporrēxī, exporrēctum, spread out (in front, from a starting-point)

ex-pugnō (1), battle down, take by storm

ex-spect-ō (1), watch for, wait for

ex-stinguō, -ere, exstīnxī, exstīnctum, put out (a fire), wipe out

ex-struō, -ere, exstrūxī, exstrūctum, heap up

ex-surgō (i.e., ex-sub-regō), -ere, exsurrēxī, exsurrēctum, raise/rise up from (a seat)

extemplō, adv., immediately

ex-tendō, -ere, extendī, extentum, stretch out, tighten up, spead out

ex-trahō, -ere, extrāxī, extrāctum, draw out

ex-trūdō, -ere, extrūsī, extrūsum, shove out

ex-urgeō, -ēre, "defective" verb, squeeze out

fābula, -ae, f., story

fābulor, -ārī, fābulātus sum, chat

faciō, -ere, fēcī, factum, make, do

fācunditās, -ātis, f., "eloquentness"

faenus, -oris, n., interest (on loan)

fallō, -ere, fefellī, falsum, deceive, trick; falsus, past pple., false, made up

famēs, -is, f., hunger

ferō, ferre, tulī/tetulī, lātum, carry, take

ferus, -a, -um, adj., wild

festīnō (1), hurry

fidēs, -ēī, f., trust, belief, faith, honesty

fīdus, -a, -um, adj., faithful

fīlia, -ae, f., daughter

fīlius, -ī, m., son

fīō, fīerī/fierī, factus sum, become (used as pass. of faciō)

foedus, -eris, n., treaty

forās/-īs, adv., out-of-doors, outside

fore, fut. infinitive of sum

foris, -is, f., door (usually pl.)

fōrma, -ae, f., form, shape

forte, adv., perhaps (= "by chance")

fortūnā-tus, -a, -um, adj., lucky; -ior, -ius, compar. adj., luckier

forum, -ī, *n.,* forum, town square

frangō, -ere, frēgī, frāctum, break

frūctus, -ūs, *m.,* fruit, reward, enjoyment

frūnīscor, -ī, frūnītus sum, have the pleasure of

frūstrā, *adv.,* "in vain"

fugiō, -ere, fūgī, run away

fugitīuos, -a, -om, *adj.* and *noun,* runaway (slave)

fugō (1), make to run away, rout

fūr, fūris, *m.,* thief

furci-fer, -ī, *m.,* slave punished by wearing "the arm-stretcher"; used as insult ("fork-carrier")

fūr-tum, -ī, *m.,* theft

garrulus, -a, -um, *adj.* and *noun,* chattering, chatterbox

gēns, -ntis, *f.,* tribe, nation; **gentium,** *gen. pl.,* "in the world"

gerō, -ere, gessī, gestum, carry, do; **rem gerō,** do the business, achieve an exploit

gest-iō, -īre, gestiī/ūī, desire, itch

gladius, -iī, *m.,* sword

glōriōsus, -a, -um, *adj.,* braggart

grānārium, -iī, *n.,* granary

grātia, -ae, *f.,* goodwill, thanks; **-ā,** *abl.,* for the sake of (**g. nostrā,** for our sake)

grātulor, -ārī, grātulātus sum, give thanks, congratulate

grau-ēdō, -inis, *f.,* headcold

grau-ida (grauis), *adj.,* pregnant ("made heavy")

gubern-ātor, -ōris, *m.,* helmsman (naturalized Greek *kubernētēs*)

gutta, -ae, *f.,* drop

habeō, -ēre, habuī, habitum, have, own

hab-itō (1), dwell in

haedus, -ī, *m.,* kid (young goat)

haereō, -ēre, haesī, haesum, stick

halo-phanta, -ae, *m.,* liar (slang: *maybe* from Greek slang, *halo-phantēs,* "harvest-exposer"?)

hāmus, -ī, *m.,* hook

haruspex, -icis (-speciō), *m.,* soothsayer who does "entrails-looking"

haud, *adv.,* not, no way

hēia, *interjection,* oh! (naturalized Greek)

hellebor-ōsus, -a, -um, *adj.,* full-of-hellebore, manic (naturalized from Greek *helleboros*)

hērcle, *"expletive" interjection,* "By Hercules!" (used all the time in chat)

heri, *adv.,* yesterday

heus, *interjection,* hey!

hic, *adv.,* here

hic, haec, hoc, *demonstrative pron.* or *adj.,* this/that

hinc, *demonstrative adv.,* from here

hircus, -ī, *m.*, billy-goat (i.e., "stink of b. o.")

hirnea, -ae, *f.*, jug

histriō, -ōnis, *m.*, actor

hōc = **hūc**

hodiē, *adv.*, today (= *hoc die*, "on this day")

homō, -inis, *m.*, human being, person

hōria, -ae, *f.*, fishing-boat

horrē-scō, -ere, "*defective*" *verb*, have hair bristle, shudder

hūc, *adv.*, to here, this way

hymēn, *m.*, the good luck chant to bless a wedding (Greek)

hymen-aeus, -ī, *m.*, the good luck chant to bless a wedding (Greek)

ī = *imperative* of **eō,** go

iaciō, -ere, iēcī, iactum, throw

iact-ō (iaciō) (1), throw around, toss

iam, *adv.*, presently, already now

ibi, *adv.*, there

ibi-dem, *adv.*, in the same place, right there

īciō, -ere, -ī, ictum, "*defective*" *verb*, strike

ī-dem, eadem, idem, *adj.* and *pron.*, the same (or the same person/thing)

id-eō, *adv.*, therefore ("that-through-that")

iēiūnitās, -ātis, *f.*, hungriness

ig-nōbilis (in-gnōbilis), -is, -e, *adj.*, not known, unknown (i.e., "nobody socially," "low-born")

ig-nōrō (in-gnōrō) (1), not know

ig-nōtus (in-gnōtus, *from* **gnōscō), -a, -um,** *adj.*, unknown; **-issumus, -a, -um,** *superl. adj.*, "unknownest"

igitur, *conj.*, therefore, so

īlicō (in locō), *adv.*, immediately ("on the spot")

ille, illa, illud, *demonstrative adj.* or *pron.*, that (over there)

il-lecebra (liciō), -ae, *f.*, lure

illi-c (ille + -ce), illaec, illuc, *demonstrative adj.* or *pron.*, that there (person or thing); **illī-c,** *adv.*, there; **illin-c,** *adv.*, from there; **illū-c,** *adv.*, to there

imāgō, -inis, *f.*, image, likeness

immō, *particle*, not in the least, "No, rather"

im-mortālis, -is, -e, *adj.*, immortal

im-mūtō (1), change, metamorphose

im-parātus, -a, -um, *adj.*, unprepared

imper-ātor, -ōris, *m.*, commander

im-percō (parcō), -ere, spare

im-perītus, -a, -um, *adj.*, inexperienced

imper-ium, -iī, *n.*, command

imperō (1), command

im-pleō, -ēre, implēuī, implētum, fill into/up

im-prānsus, -a, -um, *past pple.*, un-breakfasted

im-probus, -a, -um, *adj.*, wicked ("not-decent")

im-**pudēns**, **-ntis**, *adj.*,
shameless; -**enter**, *adv.*,
shamelessly

im-**pūrus**, **-a**, **-um**, , *adj.*,
impure, filthy

in, *prep.* + *acc.*, into/onto; *prep.*
+ *abl.*, in, on

in-**cēdō**, **-ere**, **incessī**,
incessum, proceed on

in-**cēnātus**, **-a**, **-um**, *adj.*, un-
dined

in-**cendō**, **-ere**, **incēndī**,
incēnsum, set alight

in-**cipiō** (**capiō**), **-ere**, **incēpī**,
inceptum, begin

inde, *adv.*, from here/that
moment

indic-ium, **-iī**, *n.*, pointing to,
informing on

in-**dicō** (1), point to

ind-**igēns** (**indu-egeō**), **-ntis**,
adj., needy

in-**dō**, **-ere**, **indidī**, **inditum**,
put on (with *dat.* of indirect
object)

in-**domā-bilis**, **-is**, **-e**, *adj.*,
untameable

indu-**stria** (**inde** = **in struō**),
-ae, *f.*, diligence

ind-**ūtiae** (**inde-īre**, "goings
in"), **-ārum**, *f. pl.*, truce

īnfāns, **-tīs**, *adj.* and *noun*,
child ("not-speaking")

īn-fectus, **-a**, **-um**, *adj.*, not-
done

īn-fīdus, **-a**, **-um**, *adj.*,
unfaithful

īnfumus, **-a**, **-um**, *superl. adj.*,
lowest

īn-fortūn-ium, **-iī**, *n.*,
misfortune, especially = a
beating

in-**genium**, **-iī**, *n.*, "in-born"
temperament/character/
genius

in-**grātiīs**, *adv.*, involuntarily
(from in-**grātiae**, *abl. pl.*, *f.*,
"with un-welcomenesses")

in-**grātus**, **-a**, **-um**, *adj.*,
unwelcome

in-**gredior** (**gradior**), **-ī**,
ingressus sum, set foot on,
embark on

in-**iciō** (**iaciō**), **-ere**, **iniēcī**,
iniectum, throw on/at

in-**imīcus**, **-a**, **-um**, *adj.*, hostile
("non-friendly")

in-**iūrātus**, **-a**, **-um**, *adj.*, not
having sworn, not under oath

in-**iūria**, **-ae**, *f.*, injustice,
wrong-doing

in-**lecebra** (**liciō**), **-ae**, *f.*,
enticement

inquam, **inquit**, "*defective*"
verb, say, says

īn-scendō (**scandō**), **-ere**,
īnscendī, **īnscēnsum**, climb
onto

īn-sidiae (**sedeō**), **-ārum**, *f. pl.*,
ambush

īn-spect-ō (1), take a good look
into, scan

īn-spiciō (**speciō**), **-ere**, **īnspēxī**,
īnspectum, look into

īn-stō, **-āre**, **īnstitī**, stand on

īn-struō, **-ere**, **īnstrūxī**,
īnstrūctum, put in order,
provide with, plan

in-teger, -gra, -grum, *adj.*,
whole ("untouched,
unharmed")
intel-legō, -ere, intellēxī,
intellēctum, understand
inter, *prep.* + *acc.*, among,
between
inter-ea/-im, *adv.*, meanwhile
("in-between [those
things]")
inter-ficiō, -ere, interfēcī,
interfectum, do away
with, kill (with *abl.* "of
separation," "sever from")
inter-rogō (1), question, grill
inter-uāllum, -ī, *n.*, interval (of
time or space; "the space in-
between the ramparts round
a camp")
intes-tīnum (intus), -ī, *n.*, gut
(usually *pl.* = "insides")
in-trā/-ō, *adv.*, within; *prep.* +
acc., inside
in-trō (1), enter
in-tus, *adv.*, inside
in-ueniō, -īre, inuēnī,
inuentum, come upon, find
in-uīsō, -ere, inuīsī, inuīsum,
go to see, visit
in-uocō (1), call upon
in-ūtilis, -is, -e, *adj.*, useless
iocus, -ī, *m.*, joke, prank
ipse/-us (is-pse), -a/eapse, -um,
adj. and *pron.*, the selfsame,
or him-/her-/it-self
īrācundus, -a, -um, *adj.*, angry
īrāscor, -ī, īrātus sum, am
angry
ir-rītō (1), provoke

ir-ruptiō, -ōnis, *f.*, bursting in
is, ea, id, *demonstrative adj./
pron.*, he, she, it/that
is-te, -a, -ud, *demonstrative
pron.* and *adj.*, this one
ist-īc (iste-hīc), *adv.*, over there
(in your direction)
ist-ic (iste-hic), -aec, -oc,
demonstrative pron. and *adj.*,
that one t/here (istōc, *abl.*,
"by that," on *that* account")
ist-uc (iste-ce), *adv.*, to t/here,
that way
ita, *adv.*, thus, so
item, *adv.*, likewise
i-ter (eō, īre), -ineris, *n.*,
journey
iti-dem (ita), *adv.*, in the same
way
iubeō, -ēre, iussī, iussum, order
(with *dat.*)
iū-dicō (iūs dīcō) (1), judge,
decide, sentence ("indicate
right")
iūr-ātō, *adv.*, under oath
iūrō (1), swear (an oath)
iūs, -ūris, *n.*, right
iuuentus, -ūtis, *f.*, youth, the
peer-group of young men

labellum, -ī, *n.*, lip
labōs, -ōris, *m.*, work, effort,
struggle
labr-um, -ī, *n.*, lip
lact-ō (liciō) (1), entice
lacus, -ūs, *m.*, basin, cistern
lampas, -adis, *f.*, torch,
firebrand (naturalized
Greek)

lanius, -iī, *m.*, butcher

lanterna, -ae, *f.*, lamp

lapis, -idis, *m.*, stone

larg-ior, -īrī, largītus sum, bestow big-time, hand lavish gifts to

lassus, -a, -um, *adj.*, tired

lateō, -ēre, latuī, lurk, lie low

laudō (1), praise

lectus, -ī, *m.*, bed, couch

legiō, -ōnis, *f.*, legion, military unit

legō, -ere, lēgī, lēctum, gather, "pick up"

lēna, -ae, *f.*, -ō, -ōnis, *m.*, brothel-keeper, madame/ pimp

lentus, -a, -um, *adj.*, pliant, clingy, sticky

lepidus, -a, -um, *adj.*, elegant, charming, neat

lēx, lēgis, *f.*, law

līber, -a, -um, *adj.*, free; -ē, *adv.*, -ly ; -ī, *pl.*, children or free people

līberō (1), set free (slave)

licet, -ēre, licitum est, *impers. verb*, it is allowed; although (with *subjunctive*)

līc-tor (ligō, "tie"), -ōris, *m.*, lictor (= Roman magistrate's police bodyguard)

līma, -ae, *f.*, file

līmen, -inis, *n.*, threshold

lingua, -ae, *f.*, tongue

littera, -ae, *f.*, letter (ABC); -ae, (*pl.*), letter (mail)

lītus, -oris, *n.*, shore

locō (1), place, lease, invest, lend

locus, -ī, *m.*, place

longus, -a, -um, *adj.*, long; -ē, *adv.*, far away

loquor, -ī, locūtus sum, speak, say

lōrum, -ī, *n.*, thong, lash

lubet, -ēre, lubitum est, *impers. verb*, it pleases (with *dat.*)

lubīdo, -inis, *f.*, desire

lūca bōs, -ae bouis, *f.*, elephant ("? cow")

luc-erna (lūx), -ae, *f.*, oil-lamp

lūcrum, -ī, *n.*, profit

lūdi-fico/-or, -āre/-ī, -āuī/-ātus sum, make fun of

lūdus, -ī, *m.*, game; -ī, *pl.*, the games, public festivities

lūmbi-fragium (frangō), -iī, *n.*, "back-breaking"

lūmbus, -ī, *m.*, midriff, back/ crotch

lūmen, -inis, *n.*, light

lūx, lūcis, *f.*, light; -ī, *abl.*, by day ("in the light")

macellum, -ī, *n.*, (food-)market

machaera, -ae, *f.*, dagger, short sword (naturalized Greek)

magis, *adv.*, more

mag-nus, -a, -um, *adj.*, great; ma-ior, *compar. adj.*, greater; maxumus, -a, -um, *superl. adj.*, greatest; -ē, *adv.*, in the greatest way, mostly

māla, -ae, *f.*, jaw, cheekbone

malacus, -a, -um, *adj.*, soft (naturalized Greek)

male-ficium (faciō), -iī, *n.*, wrongdoing

male-ficus (faciō), **-a**, **-um**, *adj.*, doing wrong

male-uolus, **-a**, **-um**, *adj.*, ill-willed

malus, **-a**, **-um**, *adj.*, bad, **-um**, *n.*, pain, ruination; **-e**, *adv.*, badly

maneō, **-ēre**, **mānsī**, **mānsum**, stay put, wait; **-ēdum**, *imperative*, wait a mo'

mani-pulāris, **-is**, **-e (manus)**, *m.*, non-ranking soldier ("of a handful/band of troops")

manus, **-ūs**, *f.*, hand

mare, **-is**, *n.*, sea

mari-tumus, **-a**, **-um**, *adj.*, of the sea

marītus, **-ī**, *m.*, married man, husband

mastīgia, **-ae**, *m.*, "(slave) always on the wrong end of a whip" (naturalized Greek slang *mastīgias*)

māter, **-tris**, *f.*, mother

mātrōna, **-ae**, *f.*, "Mrs." ("lady-wife-and-mother")

maxumus, *see* **magnus**

medic-īna, **-ae.**, *f.*, healing

medius, **-a**, **-um**, *adj.*, in-the-middle

mel, **mellis**, *n.*, honey

mel-culum, **-ī**, *n.*, honey-pie

melior, **-or**, **-us**, *compar. adj.*, better

membrum, **-ī**, *n.*, limb

meminī, **meminisse**, "*defective*" *verb*, remember ("have brought to mind")

memor-ātus, **-ūs**, *f.*, recounting

memor-iter, *adv.*, from memory

memorō (1), remind, mention, recount

mendāc-ium, **-(i)ī**, *n.*, lie

mendāx, **-cis**, *adj.*, lying

mēns, **-ntis**, *f.*, mind

mēnsa, **-ae**, *f.*, table

mēnsis, **-is**, *m.*, month

mentior, **-īrī**, **mentītus sum**, lie, fib

mentum, **-ī**, *n.*, chin

mercēs, **-ēdis**, *f.*, wage, price

mereō/-or, **-ēre/-ērī**, **uī/-itus sum**, earn, deserve; **meritum**, **-ī**, *n.* as *noun*, desert, reward

merus, **-a**, **-um**, *adj.*, pure, 100%; **-um**, *n.*, neat wine

metuō, **-ere**, **metuī**, **metūtum**, fear

meus, **-a**, **-um**, *adj.*, my

mīles, **-itis**, *m.*, soldier

mīlle, *numeral*, 1,000

mina, **-ae**, *f.*, Greek coin (*mna*)

minus, **-ōris**, *compar. adj.* or *noun* as *adv.*, less

minūtu-lus (minuō), **-a**, **-um**, *adj.*, teeny-weeny

mīrus, **-a**, **-um**, *adj.*, amazing

miser, **-a**, **-um**, *adj.*, wretched

mittō, **-ere**, **mīsī**, **missum**, send

mod-erō (1), control

modō, *adv.*, only, just; just now

modus, **-ī**, *m.*, measure, manner; **huius modī**, of this sort; **quem ad modum**, how ("after what fashion"); **quō modō**, how ("in what way")

molestia, -āe, *f.,* load of trouble, "drag"

moles-tus, -a, -um, *adj.,* "a drag"

monē-trīx, -īcis, *f.,* advisoress

mōn-strō (1), show

mora, -ae, *f.,* obstacle, delay

morbus, -ī, *m.,* disease

morior, -ī, mortuus sum, die

mortuālia, -ium, *n. pl.,* funeral rites, keening

mōs, mōris, *m.,* habit, way (*pl.* = "character")

moueō, -ēre, mōuī, mōtum, move

mox, *adv.,* presently

mulier, -is, *f.,* woman

multa, -ae, *f.,* fine, penalty

multi-potēns, -ntis, *adj.,* "with-manifold-powers"

multus, -a, -um, *adj.,* much, (*pl.*) many

mund-itia, -ae, *f.,* neatnesss/ cosmetics

murmurō (1), murmur

muss-itō (1), mumble

muttiō, -īre, muttīuī, mutter

nam, *conj.,* for, because

nancīscor, -ī, nactus sum, acquire

nārrō (1), tell

nāscor (i.e., **gnāscor**), **-ī, nātus sum,** am born

nāsum/-us, -ī, *n.* or *m.,* nose

nāuis, -is, *f.,* ship

nautea, -ae, *f.,* liquid gunge (naturalized Greek; lit. "seasickness")

-n(e), *interr. particle added to preceding word,* surely . . .?

nē, *conj.,* so that not, in case (with *subjunctive*)

nē, *affirmative particle,* yes indeed (naturalized Greek *nē/nai*)

nebula, -ae, *f.,* cloud

nec/neque, *negative particle,* and not; **nec . . . nec,** neither . . . nor

negō (1), deny, say no/not

negōtium (nec-ōtium), -iī, *n.,* job, business ("not-ease")

nēmo (ne-homō), -inis, *m./f. pron.,* no one

nequ-eō (neque eō), -īre, nequiī/-īuī, be unable, can't ("and not go")

nē-quiter (nē-aequiter), *adv.,* badly

nē-sciō, -īre, nēsciī/-iuī, nēscītum, not know; **nēscioquis, -is, -id,** *n.,* someone-or-other

nēu/-ue, *conj.,* and so that not/ neither/nor

nē-uis = **nōlis**

nī/nisi, *conj.,* unless, if not

nictō (1), blink, wink

ni-hil/nīl (nē-hīlum, "not-a-bit"**),** *n.,* nothing; **-ī faciō,** regard/treat as worth nothing

nimis, *adv.,* too (much), very

nimius, -a, -um, *adj.,* too, very; **-um,** *adv.,* too/very

noceō, -ēre, nocuī, nocitum, harm (with *dat.*)

noctū, *adv.* , by night (*abl.* of **nōx**)

nōlō (nē-uolō), **nōlle**, **nōluī**, not-want, refuse

nōmen, **-inis**, *n.*, name

nōminō (1), name

nōn, *adv.*, not

nōn-ne, *interr. adv.*, Isn't it the case/surely?

nōs, nostrī/-um, nōbīs, nōs, nōbīs, *pron.*, you (*pl.*)

nōscō (gnōscō), **-ere**, **nōuī**, **nōtum**, get to know

nos-ter, **-tra**, **-trum**, *adj.*, our

nōtus (nōscō), **-a**, **-um**, *adj.*, known

nouos, **-a**, **-om**, *adj.*, new

nōx, noctis, *f.*, night

nūb-ilus (nūbēs), **-a**, **-um**, *adj.*, cloudy, foggy

nūbō, **-ere**, **nūpsī**, **nūptum**, marry (usually of "the bride" = **nūpta**)

nu-diūs-quīntus (nunc dies quīntus [est], *adj.*, "now-day-five" = four days ago)

nūgae, **-ārum**, *f. pl.*, trivia, rubbish

nūg-ātor, **-ōris**, *m.*, twit, dork ("trivia-guy")

n-ūllus (nē-ūllus), **-a**, **-um**, *adj.* and *pron.*, no, no one; **nūllum**, *n.*, nothing, nowt, *adv.*, not at all

n-umquam (nē-umquam), *adv.*, never

num-quis, **-is**, **-id?** *interr. adj.* and *pron.*, not some?; not someone/thing?

nunc, *adv.*, now

nūntiō (1), announce

nūptiae (nūbō), **-ārum**, *f.*, wedding

n-ūsquam (nē-ūsquam), *adv.*, nowhere

nūt-ō (nuō) (1), do nodding

nūtrīx, **-īcis**, *f.*, wetnurse

ō, *interjection*, o, oh!

ob/obs-, *prep.* + *acc.*, on account of; *prefix* = "in the way of"

ob-ambulō (1), walk up to, walk by

ob-līuīscor, **-ī**, **oblītus sum**, forget

ob-oleō, **-ēre**, **oboluī**, smell, stink of

ob-rēpō, **-ere**, **obrēpsī**, **obrēptum**, creep up on

ob-secrō (1), beseech (in the name of what is *sacred*)

ob-sideō, **-ēre**, **obsēdī**, **obsessum**, sit on, sit out

ob-sīgnō (1), seal up

ob-temperō (1), obey (with *dat.*)

ob-truncō (1), lop (off branches), chop to pieces

ob-uāgiō, **-īre**, **obuāgīuī**, "*defective*" *verb*, bawl at

ob-ueniō, **-īre**, **obuēnī**, **obuentum**, come upon (with *dat.*)

oc-cāsiō (cadō), **-ōnis**, *f.*, opportunity ("falling-upon")

oc-cipiō (capiō), **-ere**, **occēpī**, **occeptum**, take hold of, begin

oc-clūdō (claudō), **-ere**, **occlūsī**, **occlūsum**, shut up

oc-cupō (1), seize, occupy, busy
oc-currō, -ere, occucurrī,
    occursum, run to meet
    (with *dat.*)
ocul-ātus, -a, -um, *adj.*, having
    eyes
oculus, -ī, *m.*, eye
odium, -iī, *n.*, hate, disgust
odor, -ōris, *m.*, odor
operiō, -īre, operuī, opertum,
    cover
of-fic-ium (opi-faciō), -iī, *n.*,
    duty ("help-doing")
of-flectō, -ere, "*defective*" *verb*,
    turn to face
ō-mittō (ob-), -ere, ōmīsī,
    ōmissum, let go
omnis, -is, -e, *adj*, and *pron.*,
    all, every
oper-a, -ae, *f.*, work, effort, care
opīnō/-or, opīnāre/-ārī, -āuī/
    -ātus sum, think
oportet, -ēre, oportuit, *impers.*
    verb, it is obligatory (with
    dat. of person)
op-pidum (ob-pedum, "on the
    plain"), -ī, *n.*, town
op-pleō, -ēre, opplēuī,
    opplētum, fill up
optumus, -a, -um, *adj.*, best; -ē,
    adv., in the best way
opus, -eris, *n.*, task, work; opus
    est (with *abl.*; with ut and
    subjunctive), there is a need
    (of), it is needful (to)
ōr-ātiō, -ōnis, *f.*, speech
ōrnā-mentum, -ī, *n.*, equipment
ōrō (1), pray, beg
ōs, ōris, *n.*, face

os-tendō (obs-), -ere, ostendī,
    ostentum, show
os-tent-ātor, -ōris, *m.*, show-
    off, parader
os-tent-ō (1), show off
ōstium, -iī, *n.*, door
ōti-ōsus, -a, -um, *adj.*, at ease
    ("rest-full"); -ē, *adv.*, at ease

pāc-tum (pāc-īscōr), *n.*,
    agreement, means; quō
    pāctō = "on what terms,
    how"
paene, *adv.*, almost
paenitet, -ēre, paenituit,
    impers. verb, it causes me
    regret
palam, *adv.*, openly, in the open
pall-ula, -ae, *f.*, small women's
    robe
palma, -ae, *f.*, palm (tree or
    hand)
papae, *interjection*, ow/wow!
    (naturalized Greek)
papilla, -ae, *f.*, nipple
pariō, -ere, peperī, partum,
    give birth to
parō (1), prepare,
pars, -artis, *f.*, part, share
parum, *adv.*, too little, not at all
parum-per, *adv.*, for too little
    time, briefly
pateō, -ēre, patuī, lie wide open
pater, patris, *m.*, father
patera, -ae, *f.*, bowl
patin-ārius, -a, -um, *adj.*, of a
    dish/dishes
patri-a, -ae, *f.*, fatherland
patr-ōnus, -ī, *m.*, protector

paucus, -a, -um, *adj. and noun*, little, few

paulis-per, *adv.*, for a short time

pauxillu-lus, -a, -um, *adj.*, teeny-weeny

pauxillus (paucus), -a, -um, *adj.*, teeny-tiny

pāx, -cis, *f.*, peace

peccō (1), stumble, go/do wrong

pectus, -oris, *n.*, breast, chest

pecū, *abl. of "defective" noun*, (in) a herd

pecūnia, -ae, *f.*, money

pedi-sequos, -ī, *m.*, attendant ("on foot-follower")

pel-legō, -ere, pellēgī, pellēctum, read through

pendō, -ere, pependī, pēnsum, weigh, pay out

pēnicu-lus, -ī, *m.*, sponge (and *see proper names*)

per, *prep.* + *acc.*, through, in the name of

per-dō, -ere, perdidī, perditum, destroy, lose

per-egrē (per agros, "through the fields"), *adv.*, abroad, from abroad

per-egrī-nus, -a, -um, *adj.*, from abroad, foreign

per-eō, -īre, periī, peritum, perish, go down the drain

per-iūrus, -a, -um, *adj.*, oath-breaking ("going through what's right")

per-mitiēs, -ēī, *f.*, plague

per-negō (1), keep on denying

per-petuos, -a, -om, *adj.*, continuous/-ual, for keeps

per-plexā-bilis, -is, -e, *adj.*, enigmatic ("thoroughly twisted")

pēs, pedis, *m.*, foot

pes-sum (pēs), *adv.*, to the bottom ("to the foot")

pessumus, -a, -um, *superl. adj.*, worst

petasus, -ī, *m.*, hat of traveller (naturalized Greek)

petō, -ere, petiī/īuī, petītum, attack, seek, ask

philo-sophus, -ī, *m.*, philosopher, egghead or brainiac (naturalized Greek, "friend of wisdom")

pīctūra, -ae (pīngō), *f.*, painting

piget, -ēre, piguit, *impers. verb*, it annoys

pilleum/pilleus, -ī, *n. or m.*, a felt cap, especially worn by as slave, on or after being set free

pisc-ārius, -a, -um, *adj.*, of fish/ing

piscā-tor, -ōris, *m.*, fisherman

piscis, -is, *m.*, fish

pīs-tor (pīnsō), -ōris, *m.*, miller, baker

placeō, -ēre, -uī, -itum, please (with *dat.*)

placidē, *adv.*, calmly

plānē, *adv.*, clearly; **-issumē**, *superl. adv.*, very clearly

planta, -ae. *f.*, sole of foot

platea, -ae, *f.*, boulevard, piazza (naturalized Greek) plaudō, -ere, plausī, plausum, clap

plausus, -ūs, *m.*, applause

plēnus, -a, -um, *adj.*, f

plūr-imus, -a, -um, *superl. adj.*, most ull

plūs, -ūris, *compar. adj.* or *noun* as *adv.*, more

pō-clum/pō-culum (pōtō), -ī, *n.*, drink, "glass"

poēta, -ae, *f.*, poet (naturalized Greek *poiētēs*)

pol, "*expletive*" *interjection*, "By Pollux!" (everywhere in Roman chat)

polle-ntia, -ae, *f.*, powerfulness

pōly-pus, -ī, *m.*, octopus (naturalized Greek *poulupous*, "many-footed")

pō-ne (post), *adv.* and *prep.* + *acc.*, behind

pōnō, -ere, posuī, positum, put, place

popīna, -ae, *f.*, eatery

populus, -ī, *m.*, people

porrō, *adv.*, forward, afar (naturalized Greek)

portus, -ūs, *m.*, port, harbor

poscō, -ere, poposcī, demand

possideō, -ēre, possēdī, possessum, possess

pos-sum (potis sum), posse, potuī, am able, can

post, *adv.* and *prep.* + *acc.*, after; post-eā, *adv.*, afterwards; post-illā, *adv.*, afterwards; post-quam, *conj.*, after

postulō (1), demand, insist on

pōtiō, -ōnis, *f.*, drink

potis, *n.* -e, *indecl.* or "*defective*" *adj.*, having the power, able; -ior, -ior, -ius, *compar. adj.*, more (powerful); -ius, *adv.*, more (strongly), rather; -issumus, -a, -um, *superl. adj.*, most powerful; -um, *n.* as *adv.*, especially

pōt-itō, -āre, *defective verb*, booze

pōtō, -āre, -āuī, pōtum, drink

prae-beō (habeō), -ēre, praebuī, praebitum, hold out, supply

praecō, -ōnis, *m.*, public announcer

praeda, -ae, *f.*, booty

prae-dicō (1), proclaim, declare

prae-fica, -ae, *f.*, woman hired to lead the mourning at funeral ("doing it in front")

prae-ficiō (faciō), -ere, praefēcī, praefectus, set over, put in charge of (with *dat.*)

praemium, -iī, *n.*, reward

prae-sentiō, -īre, praesēnsī, praesēnsum, feel/realize in advance

prae-sēpēs, -is, *f.*, stall, home ("fenced-off")

prae-strīngō, -ere, praestrīnxī, praestrīctum, graze, blunt

praeter, *prep.* + *acc.*, besides, apart from

prae-terō, -ere, praetrīuī, wear down (in front)

prae-ut, *conj.*, compared with the way in which

prānd-ium, -iī, *n.,* breakfast

premō, -ere, pressī, pressum, press

pretium, -iī, *n.,* reward, price

prīdem, *adv.,* before; **iam prīdem,** "long ago"

prīmō-ris, -is, -e, *adj.* and *noun,* first, foremost, "at the tip"

prīn-cip-ium (prīmus + capiō), -iī, *n.,* beginning ("first-cop")

prior, -or, -us, *compar. adj.,* earlier

prō, *interjection,* "yea!" (with *acc.*) in the name of

prō, *prep.* + *abl.,* before, in front of, instead of; **prō meīs,** "for/ as mine"

probō (1), approve (of), prove, get approval

probus, -a, -um, *adj.,* good, proper; **-ē,** *adv.,* properly

prō-cēdō, -ere, prōcessī, prōcessum, advance

procul, *adv.,* (from) afar

prō-cūrō (1), take care of

prōd-eō, -īre, prōdiī, prōditum, come forward/out

prōdest, *see* **prōsum**

proelium, -iī, *n.,* battle

pro-fectō, *adv.,* for a fact, undoubtedly

prō-ferō, prōferre, prōtulī, prōlātum, bring out

prō-fluō, -ere, prōflūxī, prōfluxum, flow out

prō-gnātus, -a, -um, *past pple. of "defective" verb,* having been born from, progeny of (with *abl.*)

prō-gredior (gradior), -ī, prōgressus sum, walk forward

pro-hibeō (habeō), -ēre, prohibuī, prohibitum, hold off, keep at bay, prevent, prohibit

prope, *adv.* and *prep.* + *acc.,* near

properō (1), hurry

prō-pīnō (1), drink to, toast (naturalized Greek)

prop-inquē, *adv.,* nearby

propitius, -a, -um, *adj.,* propitious, favorable

prop-ter, *adv.* and *prep.* + *acc.,* near

prōr-ēta, -ae, *m.,* ship's look-out ("prow-man," naturalized Greek *prōiratēs*)

prōrsus (prō-uorsus), *adv.,* turned forward, straight ahead, right on

prō-scaen-ium, -iī, *n.,* stage (naturalized Greek, "the in-front-of the backdrop")

prō-sequor, -ī, prōsecūtus sum, escort

prō-serō, -ere, *"defective" verb,* stick out

prō-sum, prōdesse, prōfuī, am of benefit to (with *dat.*)

prō-ueniō, -īre, prōuēnī, prōuentum, come forward, turn out

proxumus, -a, -um, *superl. adj.* **(prope),** nearest; **-um, -ī,** *n.,* next-door

pudīcitia, -ae, *f.,* proper sexual conduct, sense of propriety

pudīcus, -a, -um, *adj.*, properly behaved (sexually), modest
puer, -ī, *m.*, boy
pugna, -ae, *f.*, fight, battle
pugnō (1), fight
pugnus, -ī, *m.*, fist
pulchrē, *adv.*, beautifully
pult-ō (pellō) (1), knock, bash (the door)
pūniceus, -a, -um, *adj.*, crimson
pūrē, *adv.*, cleanly
purpura, -ae, *f.*, purple, purple cloth

quadrī-duum, -ī (quadri-diēs), *n.*, a four-day period
quadr-īgae (quadri-iugum), **-ārum**, *f. pl.*, four-horse team, chariot ("the four-times-yoke")
quaer-itō (1), keep seeking
quaerō, -ere, quaesiī/-īuī, quaesītum, seek
quaesō, *"defective" verb*, please ("I ask")
quaes-tus, -ūs, *m.*, profession ("seeking [a living]")
quam, *conj.*, as; than
quam-quam, *conj.*, although
quandō, *conj.*, when
quantus, -a, -um, *rel.* or *interr. adj.*, how big/as big as; **-um**, *n.* as *adv.*, as much as; **-ī**, *gen. n.* (understand **pretiī**), "for how much" ("of how big [a price]")
qua-si (quam-si), conj., as if
-que, *"enclitic" particle* (hooked onto first word in phrase/clause), and

queō, quīuī, quitum, *"defective" verb*, am able
quī, quae/qua, quod, *rel. pron.*, who, which, that
quia, *conj.*, because
quī-cum, quācum, quīcum, *rel. pron.*, with whom/which
quidem, *adv.*, indeed, even (follows the word it emphasizes)
quī-n (quī-ne), *conj.*, how/so that not ("but that"); *exclamation*, "Why!"
quīp-pe (quī), *affirmative particle*, indeed
quis, quis, quid, *interr.* or *indef. pron.*, who? what? or anyone/anything; **quid nī?**: why not?
quis-piam, quaepiam, quippiam, *indef. pron.*, anyone/thing
quis-quam, quaequam, quicquam, *indef. pron.*, any, anyone/thing)
quis-que, quaque, quodque, *indef. pron.*, each, every
quis-quis, -is, quicquid, *pron.* and *adj.*, any and anyone/thing
quī-uīs, quaeuīs, quoduīs, *adj.*, any(-you-want); **quiduīs, quoiusuīs**, *n.*, anything-you-like, whatever
quō, *conj.*, so that (with *subjunctive*); **quō?** *interr. adv.*, to where?
quoi, *dat.* of **quis**
quōius, *interr. adj.*, of whom/whose

quom (= **cum**), *conj.*, when/ since/though

quon-iam, *conj.*, since

quoque, *adv.*, too, also (after the word it modifies)

quot, *indecl. adj.*, how many/as many

quotī-diē, *adv.*, on each day

rādō, -ere, rāsī, rāsum, shave

rā-menta (**rādō**), **-ae**, *f.*, shaving, shred

rapt-ō (**rapiō**) (1), seize, plunder

rārē, *adv.*, rarely

ratiō, -ōnis, *f.*, reasoning

ratus, *see* **reor**

re-cipiō (**capiō**), **-ere, recēpī, receptum**, receive, accept

re-creō (1), re-make, refresh

rēct-ē, *adv.*, rightly

red-dō, -ere, reddidī, redditum, return, pay back

red-eō, -īre, rediī, reditum, return

re-ferō, referre, rettulī, relātum, bring back

rē-fert (*abl.* of **rēs** + **ferō**), **rēferre, rētulit**, *impers. verb*, it matters (to) (with **meā/ tuā**)

rēgīna, -ae, *f.*, queen

rēg-nō (1), rule

re-licu-os (**linquō**), **-a, -om**, *adj.*, remaining, left

religiō-sus, -a, -um, *adj.*, under a religious taboo

re-linquō, -ere, relīquī relīctum, leave (behind)

remelīgō, -inis, *f.*, hold-up

re-mittō, -ere, remīsī, remissum, send back, let go

re-moror, -ārī, remorātus sum, delay

reor, rērī, ratus sum, think

re-periō, -īre, -repperī, -tum (**pariō**), find, discover, obtain

rēs, reī, *f.*, thing, deed; **ab rē**, "away from/not in one's interests"

re-sīdō (**sedeō**), **-ēre, resēdī**, sit back, stay sitting

rē-spondeō, -ēre, respondī, respōnsum, reply

rēte, -is, *n.* or *m.*, net

re-ticeō (**taceō**), **-ēre, reticuī**, keep silent

re-tineō (**teneō**), **-ēre, retinuī, retentum**, hold back, retain

re-trahō, -ere, retrāxī, retrāctum, drag back

re-ueniō, -īre, reuēnī, reuentum, come back, return

rēx, -gis, *m.*, ruler, king

rīdeō, -ēre, rīsī, rīsum, laugh

rogō (1), ask

rōstrum (**rōdō**), **-ī**, *n.*, beak, snout

rota, -ae, *f.*, wheel

rūdēns, -ntis, *m.*, rope ("braying")

rūs, -ūris, *n.*, countryside; **-rī**, *locative*, in the country

sacer, -cra, -crum, *adj.*, sacred

saepe, *adv.*, often

saltem, *adv.*, at least, at any rate

salūbriter, *adv.*, healthily ("conducive-to-being well-ishly")

saluē, *imper.* of "*defective*" *verb*, (say) hello

saluos, **-a**, **-om**, *adj.*, safe

salūs, **-ūtis**, *f.*, safety, well-being

salūtō (1), greet, say hello

sānus, **-a**, **-um**, *adj.*, healthy, sane; **-ē**, *adv.*, soundly, truly, to be sure

sapiō, **-ere**, **sapīuī**, have a taste, smell, smell of, have (a) sense (of); **sapiēns**, **-ntis**, *adj.*, being smart, wise

sat/satis, *adv.* and *noun*, enough; **sati-us est**, *impers. verb*, it is better

sat-ur, **-a**, **-um**, *adj.*, full

sāuium, **-iī**, *n.*, kiss

scaena, **-ae**, *f.*, stage (naturalized Greek)

sceles-tus, **-a**, **-um**, *adj.* and *noun*, criminal

scelus, **-eris**, *n.*, crime; in use as insult

scī-licet (**scīre licet**), *particle*, for sure ("one can know")

sciō, **-īre**, **scīuī**, **scītum**, know

scītus (**scī-scō**), **-a**, **-um**, *adj.*, wised up, clued in, smart

scortum, **-ī**, *n.*, whore, of either sex (lit. "hide," "pelt")

scriblīta, **-ae**, *f.*, cheesy dough

scrībō, **-ere**, **scrīpsī**, **scrīptum**, write

scurra, **-ae**, *m.*, jokester

sē/sē-sē, *reflex. pron. sing.* and *pl.*, him/her/itself and them/theirselves

sed, *conj.*, but

sedeō, **-ēre**, **sēdī**, **sessum**, sit

sē-gregō (1), separate, exclude ("remove from herd")

semper, *adv.*, always

senex, **-is**, *m.*, senior citizen

sēns-im, *adv.*, gradually

sententia, **-ae**, *f.*, opinion

sentiō, **-īre**, **sēnsī**, **sēnsum**, feel, think

sepul-crum, **-ī**, *n.*, grave

seques-ter, **-tra/-tris**, **-trum/-tre**, *adj.* and *noun*, (of a) third-party holding disputed property pending settlement; **-trum**, *n.*, such safekeeping (*dat.*, **-tro ponō**, put in trust)

sequor, **-ī**, **secūtus sum**, follow

sēri-ō, *adv.*, seriously

ser-mō, **-ōnis**, *m.*, talk, chat

ser-tum (**serō**), **-ī**, *n.*, garland

seruō (1), save, keep safe

seruos, **-ī**, *m.*, slave

sex, *numeral*, six

sī, *conj.*, if

sīc, *adv.*, so, like this

siem = **sim**, *subjunctive* of **sum**

sīgnum, **-ī**, *n.*, sign, signal

sileō, **-ēre**, **siluī**, am silent

similis, **-is**, **-e**, *adj.*, like (in Plautus, with *gen.*)

simul, *adv.*, at the same time

simulō (1), imitate, pretend

sine, *prep.* + *abl.*, without

sinō, **-ere**, **sīuī**, **situm**, let, allow

siquidem, *conj.*, if in fact

sīs = sī uīs, please (if you will, **uolō**)

sitiō, -**īre**, **sitiī**/-**īuī**, thirst

socius, -**a**, -**um**, *adj.* and *m./f./n.*, sharing in; ally, partner

sōl/Sōl, -**is**, *m.*, sun/sun god

soleō, -**ēre**, **solitus sum**, am accustomed

soluō, -**ere**, **soluī**, **solūtum**, loose, set free, launch (a ship)

sōlus, -**a**, -**um**, *adj.*, alone

sōspēs, -**itis**, *adj.*, safe

spect-ātor, -**ōris**, *m.*, spectator (in the audience)

spect-ō (1), watch

specul-or, -**ārī**, **speculātus sum**, watch, spy

specu-lum, -**ī**, *n.*, mirror

spērō (1), hope (for)

spolium, -**iī**, *n.*, booty

sponte, *abl. f.*, voluntarily ("with volition")

spurcus, -**a**, -**um**, *adj.*, filthy

squāma, -**ae**, *f.*, scale

squām-ōsus, -**a**, -**um**, *adj.*, scaly

stat-ūra (**stō**), -**ae**, *f.*, height, size

sternō, -**ere**, **strāuī**, **strātum**, strew

stimulō (1), whip, urge on

stip-ulor (**stips**, "donation"), -**ārī**, **stipulātus sum**, covenant, agree terms

stō, -**āre**, **stetī**, **statum**, stand

strēnuus, -**a**, -**um**, *adj.*, energetic, urgent

stru-īx, -**īcis**, *f.*, built-up pile

stult-itia, -**ae**, *f.*, foolishness

stultus, -**a**, -**um**, *adj.*, **foolish**; -**ē**, *adv.*, foolishly

suādeō, -**ēre**, **suāsī**, **suāsum**, advise, urge

suāuis, -**is**, -**e**, *adj.*, sweet

sub, *prep.* + *abl.*, under

sub-dolus, -**a**, -**um**, *adj.*, a bit cunning

sub-igit-ātiō, -**ōnis** (**ag-itō**), *f.*, "ride-ificating," i.e.,"covering (as bull does cow)," especially "deflowering (a virgin)"

sub-itus, -**a**, -**um**, *adj.*, sudden; -**ō**, *adv.*, suddenly

sub-sellium (**sedeō**), -**iī**, *n.*, seat

suffundō, -**ere**, **suffūdī**, **suffūsum**, pour from underneath, spread through

sum, **esse**, **fuī**, **futūrus sum**, am

sum-mus (**super**), -**a**, -**um**, *adj.*, uppermost, highest

sūmō (**sub** + **emō**), -**ere**, **sūmpsī**, **sūmptum**, take up

super/-ā/suprā, *prep.* + *acc.*, over, above

superō (1), overcome

super-stēs (**stō**), -**itis**, *adj.*, surviving ("standing over")

sup-pōnō, -**ere**, -**posuī**, -**positum**, place under (cover), sneak in, substitute

sup-posit-iō, -**ōnis**, *f.*, under-cover substitution

sura, -**ae**, *f.*, calf (lower leg)

su-rgō (**sub-regō**), -**ere**, **surrēxī**, **surrēctum**, rise, get up

suspīciō, -**ōnis**, *f.*, suspicion

sȳco-phanta, -ae, *m.*, informer, slanderer/flatterer (Greek slang, *suko-phantēs*, "fig-exposer")

sym-bola, -ae, *f.*, contribution to a feast (naturalized Greek)

syn-graphus, -ī, *m.*, contract (naturalized Greek)

tabernā-clum, -ī, *n.*, tent ("hutlet")

tabula, -ae, *f.*, wood tablet (for writing on)

taceō, -ēre, tacuī, tacitum, am silent; tacitus, -a, -um, *adj.*, silent

tālus, -ī, *m.*, die ("knucklebone/anklebone")

tam, *conj.*, so, in such a way

tamen, *adv.*, however

tan-dem, *adv.*, at length

tangō, -ere, tetigī, tāctum, touch

tant-illus, -a, -um, *adj.*, *that* little

tan-tus, -a, -um, *adj.*, *that* great

tē-la (texō), -ae, *f.*, web (on a loom)

temperō (1), mix well, moderate, control

tempestās, -ātis, *f.*, storm

temptō (1), try

tenāx, -ācis, *adj.*, tenacious

tenebrae, -ārum, *f. pl.*, darkness

teneō, -ēre, tenuī, tentum, hold, grasp

tergum, -ī, *n.*, hide, back

terminus, -ī, *m.*, boundary, limit

terra, -ae, *f.*, land

testis, -is, *m.*, witness

tībī-cen (canō), -inis, *m.*, player on the oboe

tīnniō, -īre, tinniī/-īuī, tīnnītum, jingle, ring

tollō, -ere, sustulī, sublātum, lift, remove

tondeō, -ēre, totondī, tōnsum, crop, cut hair, shave

tot, *adv.*, so many

tōtus, -a, -um, *adj.*, whole, all

trāct-ō (1), handle

trag-oediā, -iae, *f.*, tragedy (naturalized Greek)

trāgula, -ae, *f.*, dragnet; -am iniciō, set a trap for (with *dat.*)

trahō, -ere, trāxī, trāctum, drag

trāns-legō, trānslegere, "*defective*" *verb*, read across (to someone else)

tre-centī, -ae, -a, *numeral*, three hundred

tri-ōbolum, -ī, *n.*, a Greek coin ("threepenny piece")

trīticum (terō, "rub"), -ī, *n.*, corn ("threshed" grain)

tū, tuī, tibi, tē/tēd, tē, *pron.*, you (*sing.*)

tum, *adv.*, then

tunica, -ae, *f.*, tunic, under-garment and/or everyday dress (often worn more than one at a time)

turbi-dus, -a, -um, *adj.*, stormy

tūs, -ūris, *n.*, frankincense (naturalized Greek *thuos*)

tussiō, -īre, *"defective" verb*, cough

tuus, -a, -um, *adj.*, your (*sing.*)

uāh, *interjection*, aha! (naturalized Greek)

ualentu-lus, -a, -um, *adj.*, strong-little-thing

ualeō, -ēre, ualuī, am well or strong, fare well

uāni-loquos, -a, -om, *adj.*, empty-talking

uāpulō (1), take a beating (a cruel slave-owner's term, as if the slave subject were the agent of his own punishment)

uariō (1), change, turn into different colors (i.e., "black and blue")

uās, -āsis, *n.*, container

ubi/-ī, *conj.*, when/where

uehementer, *adv.*, strongly, energetically

uel, *adv.*, or, either; even

uēn-alis (uēnum), -is, -e, *adj.*, for sale

uēn-ātus, -ūs, *m.*, hunting

uēnd-itō (uēndō) (1), sell, flog

uēn-dō (uēnum dō), -ere, uēndidī, uēnditum, sell

uenē-ficus (faciō), -ī, *m.*, sorcerer, poisoner

uēn-eō (uēnum eō), -īre, uēniī, am sold

ueniō, -īre, uēnī, uentum, come

uerberō (1), beat, whip

uerbum, -ī, *n.*, word; **uerba dō**, fool (with *dat.*)

uēr-culum, -ī, *n.*, "Springsie"

uērus, -a, -um, *adj.*, true; **-ē/-ō**, *adv.*, truly, **-um**, *conj.*, but, yet (lit. "truly"); (it's) true

uestiō, -īre, uestiī/-īuī, uestītum, clothe

uestītus, -ūs, *m.*, clothing

uetō, -āre, uetuī, uetitum, forbid

uetus, -eris, *adj.*, old

uia, -ae, *f.*, road, path

uīc-īnus, -a, -um, *adj.* and *noun*, neighbor/ing

uict-rīx, īcis, *f.*, victoress

uīcus, -ī, *m.*, street, neighborhood

uideō, -ēre, uīdī, uīsum, see; **-or**, *pass.*, seem

uīdulus, -ī, *m.*, trunk, chest

uigilō (1), stay awake

uīgintī, *numeral*, twenty

uīlicus, -ī, *m.*, slave estate-manager ("villa-guy")

uīlla, -ae, *f.*, villa, farm-house/house in the country

uīn = uīs-ne, do you want (**uolō**)

uinciō, -īre, uīnxī, uīnctum, bind

uinc-lum/uincu-lum (uinciō), -ī, *n.*, bond

uincō, -ere, uīcī, uictum, conquer, win

uīnum, -ī, *n.*, wine

uir, -ī, *m.*, man, warrior; husband

uirga, -ae, *f.*, twig, cane

uirtūs, -ūtis, *f.*, (male) heroism, courage

uīs, -is, *f.*, force, violence

uīs-ō, -ere, uīsī, uīsum, visit, go to see

uīta, -ae, *f.*, life

uiti-ōsus, -a, -um, *adj.*, flawed ("flaw-full")

uitium, -iī, *n.*, flaw, folly, vice

uītō (1), avoid

uī-tor (uieō), -ōris, *m.*, basket-weaver

uīuō, -ere, uīxī, uīctum, live

uīuos, -a, -om, *adj.*, alive, living

uix, *adv.*, scarcely, with difficulty

ūllus, -a, -um, *adj.* and *noun*, any, any one

ultrō, *adv.*, to the far side, beyond, besides, going further than (should be/obliged to)

ultumus, -a, -um, *adj.*, farthest

ūmor, -ōris, *m.*, liquid, water

unde, *conj.*, from where

ungu-entum, -ī, *n.*, ointment, perfume

unguō, -ere, ūnxī, ūnctum, oil, daub

ūni-cus, -a, -um, *adj.*, one-and-only, one-off

ūnus, -a, -um, *adj.*, one; **ūnā**, *adv.*, at one time, together

uocō (1), call (to), invite

uolō, uelle, uoluī, want, am willing

uolup, *adv.*, with pleasure; **u. faciō**, give pleasure to (with *dat.*)

uolup-tās, -ātis, *f.*, pleasure

uorsō (uortō) (1), keep turning

uōs, uostrī/-um, uōbīs, uōs, uōbīs, *pron.*, you (*pl.*)

uoster, -tra, -trum, *possessive adj.* or *pron.*, your (*pl.*)

uōx, -cis, *f.*, voice

urbānus, -a, -um, *adj.*, citified, sophisticated

ūs-piam, *adv.*, somewhere

ūs-que, *adv.*, all the way

ūsus, -ūs, *m.*, use, (in Roman law) claim to ownership through continuous occupation or possession.

ut/utī, *conj.*, in order that or although (with *subjunctive*,); as/how/when (with *indicative*)

uterus, -ī, *m.*, womb

ut nē, *conj.* = *nē*, so that not (with *subjunctive*)

uti-nam, *conj.*, how I wish that (with *subjunctive*)

ut-ut, *indef. conj.*, howsoever (with *indicative*)

ūuidus, -a, -um, *adj.*, wet

uxor, uxōris, *f.*, wife

uxōr-cula, -ae, *f.*, wifey

Proper Names

∾ (with their English naturalized forms)
Guide to the English Pronunciation

Achillēs, -is, *m.*, Achilles.
Greek *Achilleus,* "The Pain
Man," with hints of "The
Achaean," i.e., "The Greek."
AKH-ILL-EEZ.

Agorasto-clēs, -is, *m.*,
Agorastocles. Greek
Agorasto-klēs, "Marketing-
famous." **A-GOR-AST-OK-
LEEZ.**

Alcēsimarchus, -ī, *m.*,
Alcesimarchus. Greek
**Alkēsim-archos,*
"Mighteous-ruler." **AL-
KEEZ-IM-AR-KHUS.**

Alcumēna, ae, *f.*, Alcmena.
Greek *Alkmēnē,* "Mighty-on
the Warpath"? **ALK-MEE-
NA.**

Amphi-truō, -ōnis, *m.*,
Amphitryō. Greek
Amphitruōn, "All-around-
Harrassing"? **AM-FIT-REE-
OH.**

Ārabia, -ae, *f.*, Arabia. **A-RAY-
BI-A.**

Arist-archus, -ī, *m.*, Aristarchus.
Greek *Aristarchus,* "Best-
ruler" / "Best-Starter."
ARRISS-TARKH-US.

Astaphium, -iī, *n.*, Astaphium.
Greek *Astaphion,* "Raisin-
ette." **A-STA-FI-UM.**

Athēnāe, -ārum, *f.*, Athens.
A-THENZ.

Atticus, -a, -um, *adj.*, Attic (of
Athens' territory of Attica).
AT-TICK.

Calli-phō, -ōnis, *m.*, Callipho.
Greek *Kalliphōn,* "Beauty-
Shiner"? **CAL-LI-FOE.**

Casina, -ae, *f.*, Casina. Hints
of "Girl from Casīnum"
(a town near Rome) /
"Cinnamon Girl" (from
casia?). **CAZ-IN-A.**

Castor, -oris, *m.*, Castor. Minor
deity. Greek *Kastōr.* **KASS-
TOR.**

Cereālis, -is, -e, *adj.*, of Ceres,
Cereal. Goddess of grain.
SEAR-EE-AL.

Chalīnus, -ī, *m.,* Chalinus.
Greek slave name, "bit,
curb" (for equid, or human
donkey). **KHA-LEE-NUS.**

Chor-āgus, -ī, *m.,* theater
manager. Greek *chorēgos,*
"Chorus Leader." **KHO-RAY-
GUS.**

Cle-āreta, -ae, *f.,* Cleäreta.
Greek *kle-aretē,* "Glory-
Excellence." **CLEE-A-RET-A.**

Cleu-strata, -ae, *f.,* Cleustrata.
Greek *kleo-stratē,* "Glory-
Army." **CLUE-STRA-TA.**

Cloācīna, -ae, *f.,* Cloacina.
Roman purification deity
associated with Venus,
hooked onto **cloāca,** "main
drain." **CLO-AH-KEEN-A.**

Collybiscus, -ī, *m.,* Collybiscus.
Greek slave name,
Kollubiskos, "Dime-y" or
"Penny-let." **COL-LIB-ISK-US.**

Cupīdō, -inis, *m.,* Cupid. God
of **cupīdō, -inis,** *f.,* desire/
lust. **CUE-PID.**

Dāuos, -ī, *m.,* Davus. Slave
name naturalized from
Greek *Dāos.* **DAH-WUS.**

Dia-bolus, -ī, *m.,* Diabolus. Greek
dia-bolos, "Mud-Slinger/
Snitch." **DEE-AB-OL-US.**

Erōtium, -iī, *n.,* Erotium. Greek
Erōtion, "Aimée/Sex-kitten."
E-ROE-TI-UM.

Euthy-nīcus, -ī, *m.,* Euthynicus.
Greek *Euthynīkos,*
"Straightahead Victor."
YOU-THIN-EYE-KUS.

Glaucus, -ī, *m.,* Glaucus.
Greek name, recurrent
in mythology, *Glaukos,*
"Gleaming/Grey." In
comic mockery, hinting at
glaukōma, "cataract," i.e.,
an eye-disease to do with
envious casting of the evil
eye? **GL-OW!-CUS.**

Grīpus, -ī, *m.* Gripus. Greek
"Catch (of fish)" / "Basket
(or fish)," punning with
Greek *grīpos/grīphos,* riddle?
GREE-PUS.

Histri-cus, -a, -um, *adj.,* of
Istria (coastal Slovenia).
Punning as if from **histrio,**
"of an actor." **IST-RICK-US.**

Homēr-onidā, -ae, *m.,*
Homeronides. Mock Greek
name for soldier who blows
his own trumpet, "Homer-
son" / "One of the Homer
Clan." **HOE-MER-ONI-DEEZ.**

Iup-piter, Iouis, *m.,* Jupiter,
"god the Father." **JOO-PI-TA.**

Leucadius, -a, -um, *adj.,* from
Leucadia (on the coast of
northwestern Greece). **LŪ-
KĀD-I-A.**

Lȳsi-dāmus, -ī, *m.,* Lysidamus.
Greek "Free-da-People."
LIE-SI-DAME-US.

Mārs, -ārtis, *m.,* Mars. Roman
god of war. **MARZE.**

Men-aechmus, -ī, *m.,*
Menaechmus. Greek
menaichmēs, "Steady-under-
Spears." **MEN-IKE-MUS.**

Merc-urius, -iī, *m.*, Mercury. "God of trade." **MER-KUR-I-US.**

Milphiō, -ōnis, *m.*, Milphio. Greek slave name, *Milphiōn*, "Eyelashy." **MIL-FI-OH.**

Neriēnis, -is, *f.*, Nerienis. Roman goddess, wife of Mars. **NE-RI-AY-NIS.**

Olympiō, -onis, m., Olympio. Greek slave name, *Olumpiōn*, "Heaven-ite." **O-LIM-PI-OH.**

Oppia, -ae, *f.*, Oppia, female member of the family Oppia. **OP-PI-A.**

Pardal-isca, -ae, *f.*, Pardalisca. Greek, "Sweet Baby Panther." **PARD-AL-ISK-A.**

Pēni-culus (pēnis), -ī, *m.*, Peniculus (nickname "Brushkin/Sponge-let," punning with "Prick-let." **PEA-NICK-U-LUS.**

Pers-icus, -a, -um, *adj.*, from Persia/Iran. Punning with "of Perseus, King of Macedon"? **PER-SICK-US.**

Phaedromus, -ī, *m.*, Phaedromus. Greek name from *phaidros*, "Gleaming." **FIE-DRO-MUS.**

Phil-aenium, -iī, *n.*, Philaenium. Greek *Phil-ainion*, "Loves-Praise-ette" / "Likes-a-Tale-let" / "Kissing-to-Rhapsodize-Over-ine." **FILL-IGH-NI-UM.**

Phil-ippus, -ī, *m.*, "a Philip." Macedonian gold coin. **FI-LIP.**

Phronēsium, -iī, *n.*, Phronesium. Greek *Phronesion*, "Ms./Dear Prudence-ine." **FRON-EE-ZI-UM.**

Phrygia, -ae, *f.*, Phrygia (in Turkey, a region of central and west Asia Minor). **FRIDG-I-A.**

Plautīnus, -a, -um, *adj.*, Plautine, of Plautus. **PLAW-TINE** or **OF PLAW-TUS.**

Pontus, -i, *m.*, Pontus, the Black Sea. Greek *pontos*, "sea." **PON-TUS.**

Pro-logus, -ī, *m.*, Prologue, introducer / introduction. Greek *pro-logos.* **PRO-LOG-US.**

Pseudolus, -ī, *m.*, Pseudolus. Slave name from Greek *pseudō*, "cheat, trick, lie." **PSU-DO-LUS.**

Pterela, -ae, *m.*, Pterelas. Greek royal name, "Winged-one (. . . of the people?)." **PTE-REL-A.**

Sīmō, -ōnis, *m.*, Simon. Greek *Sīmōn*, "Snub-Nose-y." **SIGH-MOH.**

Sōsia, -ae, *m.*, Sosia. Greek *Sōsias*, slave's speaking name, "Savior," so "Still Alive." **SOH-ZI-A.**

Strato-phanēs, -is, *m.*, Stratophanes. Greek "Army-Fantasist," i.e., paper tiger. **STRA-TO-FA-NEEZ.**

Syria, -ae, *f.*, Syria. **SI-RI-YA.**

Syrus, -a, -um, *adj.*, Syrian. **Si-ri-an.**

Tēle-boāe, -ārum, *m.*, Teleboans. A tribe of pirates in northwest Greece, "The Far-Yellers." **Tee-leb-oh-ans.**

Thalēs, -is, *m.*, Thales. A legendary Wise Man, Greek "Bloomer." As a sneer at a brainiac, "Einstein!" **Thay-leez.**

Thēbānus, -a, -um, *adj.*, Theban; *m.*, = "citizen of the Greek city Thēbes." **Thee-ban.**

Trachāliō, -ōnis, *m.*, Trachalio. Greek slave name from *trachēlos*, "Neck-let," i.e., "Scruff-of-Neck" or "The One with the Neck" (always wearing the yoke, or punished with the neck-brace). **Tra-khar-leo.**

Tuscus, -a, -um, *adj.*, Etruscan. **Tuss-kus.**

Vēlābrum, -ī, *n.*, Velabrum. Market district in Rome. **Vee-lahb-rum.**

Venus, -eris, *f.*, Venus. Goddess of love/sex. **Vee-nus.**